GUNDOG TRAINING

GUNDOG
TRAINING

Your Problems Solved!

J. C. Jeremy Hobson

B. T. Batsford Ltd · London

For everyone interested in understanding dogs in general and gundogs in particular. Also to my Father with thanks for his encouragement, help and support in all my interests and activities.

© J. C. Jeremy Hobson 1993
First published 1993

Typeset by Servis Filmsetting Ltd, Manchester
and printed and bound in Great Britain by
Butler and Tanner, Frome, Somerset
for the publishers
B. T. Batsford Ltd
4 Fitzhardinge Street
London W1H 0AH

A CIP catalogue record for this book is available from the British Library
ISBN 0 7134 6941 2

By the same author:
Beagling (David & Charles, 1987)
Small-Scale Game Rearing (The Crowood Press, 1988)
What Every Gun Should Know (David & Charles, 1989)
Working Terriers (The Crowood Press, 1989)
Cultivating a Shoot (David & Charles, 1991)

Line-drawings by Clare E. Pavey

CONTENTS

ACKNOWLEDGEMENTS

It is neither my nor my publisher's intention to produce a general training manual – there are many such already on the market. You will not, therefore, find any of the initial steps included within these pages. You will, however, discover, in an A to Z format, all of the problems likely to be encountered once basic training has commenced.

The various topics and subsequent headings have come about as a result of discussions between myself and professional trainers, all of whom need to be successful in order to make a living. Although I must accept the fact that, when dealing with livestock, one can never fail to learn something new every day, I nevertheless feel that experience leads them to know most, if not all of the answers and it is because of their wish to upgrade gundog standards that they have given their time freely. Their help in the production of this book is, therefore, greatly appreciated. They

are: Mr 'Sam' Seall of Orchard Cottage, Bereleigh, East Meon, Petersfield, Hampshire; Mr Richard Webb of Birdbrook Gundogs, Ness Road, Burwell, Cambridgeshire; and Mr Ron Seal of Rillon Gundogs & Demonstrations, Garage Flat, Linch Gate House, Linch, near Liphook, Hampshire.

Thanks must also go to Gina Arnold for her invaluable assistance in transforming my very rough 'longhand' into a readable manuscript. Being of a very versatile nature, her photographs have also appeared on several pages.

Clare Pavey has, for the third time of asking, agreed to help with the line-drawings. Her attention to detail and obvious interest in dogs has resulted in some excellent work, for which she has my sincere thanks.

Finally, my thanks to Faber & Faber Ltd for permission to quote from *Spaniels For Sport* by Talbot Radcliffe.

INTRODUCTION

It is a well-known fact that you can, without fear of recrimination, criticize a particular neighbour in their choice of interior decor, car or potential holiday destination. A wife/husband or their children's behaviour will often go without comment as will any reference towards their own shortcomings. Criticize his gundog, however, and you are likely to lose a friend.

After some 20 years' gamekeeping experience (during which time I must admit to having made my own share of training failures and mishaps), I have to say that I have seen more average and mediocre shooting dogs than those which were outstandingly brilliant. With a little help and advice from those who were afraid to give constructive criticism for fear of giving offence, I have no doubt that some of these dogs could have been improved, giving more enjoyment to the owner and greater fulfilment to the dog.

Within the pages of this book, I therefore intend to play devil's advocate, throwing the potential problems and queries at professional trainers in an effort to arrive at the best, sometimes conflicting, advice. Read it as a training manual and you

will, I fear, be missing out on the basics. There are many excellent publications dealing with a gundog's formative training already on the bookshelves. Use it as a reference when problems occur, however, and it will offer some sound help and advice.

There is no point in thinking that you do not require one of 'those circus dogs you see at field trials which haven't got the brains to think for themselves and need directing by a chap throwing two arms about like a demented windmill, at the same time as he blows a mouthful of whistles'! Everyone, no matter what their chosen type of shooting, needs a dog trained to a certain standard. Admittedly, the potential Field Trial Champion needs to be more 'polished' than the rough-shooter's, but even his dog needs to stop on command and work within gun-shot range if the handler is to stand any chance of firing a cartridge.

Pigeon shooting on the stubbles can be made impossible if, every time a shot is fired and a bird falls, your retriever departs to the farthest reaches of the field, taking with it hide poles and camouflage net. Beaters and pickers-up, whilst perhaps more interested in dog work

Everyone needs a dog trained to a certain standard.

rather than in shooting itself, would not find many shoots keen to offer them a day out if they had not troubled with a certain amount of basic training. To the gamekeeper a shooting day is, after all, his only chance of proving his worth to his employer and a spaniel, rushing forward and flushing birds indiscriminately, is not going to help towards achieving a record season.

As will be seen when reading this book, problems can occur at any time and with a dog of any age. Never, therefore, be lulled into a false sense of security by that perfectly trained paragon of virtue sitting at your feet as you read this. If you have accepted

that you have not the patience or aptitude to train a dog yourself, you may have been persuaded to buy a professionally-trained dog. Again, do not be fooled for one moment into thinking that the hours of training already invested in your dog means that you do not have to be careful that he does not slip into bad habits.

It is an unfortunate fact that many professional people fall into the trap of assuming that once a retriever is bought from a reliable trainer, it will remain for all time a tried and trusted ally both on and off the shooting field. In reality, no matter how much money you are prepared to spend, without constant handling even the best-trained dog will revert to negative behaviour. A stagshorn whistle may well have been given to you with the dog but without some 'insider' knowledge to its use, it may just have well remained in the trainer's pocket.

The prime cause of problems occurring is a lack of understanding between dog and handler. The classic example, undoubtedly noticed by all reading this book, is where a dog runs in only to be thrashed with a lead or stick upon its return. To the handler, it is just punishment for the act of running-in but to the dog, he is being chastised for his last act and that is returning to the handler. Next time he will obviously be reluctant to return, fearing more of the same treatment.

He may well cause more trouble and embarrassment, perhaps working on the human theory that he 'may as well be hung for a sheep as a lamb'.

Never, ever, be tempted to vent your anger on the dog. Beating him will only result in a lack of trust, and thinking that it is possible to show just who is 'boss' by such action is doomed to failure. An oft-quoted maxim states, 'A wife, a spaniel and a walnut tree / the more you beat them / the better they'll be'. In following this maxim you are no better than the Victorian dog breakers who, quite literally, let a pupil run riot and then attempted to instil discipline by means

Successful gundog training is dependent upon understanding and a desire to please. These dogs are completely attentive to their handler.

of a stick. From an initial intake of, say, ten dogs, perhaps two could make the grade, the remainder being disposed of via the gun.

Successful gundog training involves much more than this. It is a question of psychology and understanding, not brute force and ignorance. Any advice and guidance whether in this book or another is merely that and should not be taken as gospel: the fact that it is written that training for the average gundog takes six months does not necessarily mean that you should immediately pass on to the finer points of training without having first instilled the basics after this period of time. If in doubt, begin again and this time, take things more slowly. A well-trained gundog will be an acceptable and happy shooting companion for around eight to ten years and so it is obviously a short-sighted act to rush its training.

During my research for this book, the comment 'return to basics when necessary' has appeared more than once and so I make no apology for offering the same advice in several of the problem sections.

A

ADVICE

This is my first attempt at training a gundog. I've read all the books but some trainers tell me to do it one way, others another. On top of this a shooting friend suggested that I should ignore them all and use my common sense. I don't want to ruin my dog, which is progressing well, but know that I shall need help and advice sooner or later.

As with any learning process, nothing can substitute help from a gundog owner with a lifetime's experience and knowledge. Professional advice is bound to be better than that offered by friends, no matter how well-meaning, as a trainer needs to have found out all the right solutions in order to make a living from his chosen career. Because of their interest in the long-term well-being of gundogs, they are, fortunately, only too happy to divulge some of their secrets.

Failing the assistance of a local professional, it will pay to join a gundog club. There are many such clubs throughout the country. Some cater for a single breed; others are more general, working with a wide variety of types and breeds of gundog.

Almost all of these are affiliated to the Kennel Club who should be able to provide a list of club names and their secretaries.

Sometimes, however, a local gundog enthusiast will set up a small organization, the main objective of which is to provide training sessions, and perhaps also group social activities. This will probably not have any connection with the Kennel Club and you will have to use your powers of detection in order to locate a contact.

Once you have found a club which answers all your requirements, joining is a simple matter. A proposer and seconder are normally required and an annual subscription is levied which, in most cases, is not more than a few pounds. Some clubs will not, however, accept membership from would-be members living outside the given area. Others are so popular that they have a waiting-list.

As well as being able to obtain good advice from newly-made and experienced friends on a general basis, training classes and gundog tests give the novice trainer the opportunity both to learn through practice and gain confidence working in public. The latter is obviously very important to those readers whose ultimate aim is to compete at field trials. As you might imagine, it would be most embarrassing to train a gundog to perfection in the peace and quite of the home environment only to have him run wild with excitement out in company.

TRAINERS' TIPS

- Contact a professional gundog trainer or your local gundog club.

- It is best to contact a professional gundog trainer who has been in the business for some years, has had experience of all breeds of gundog and has a good track record.

AGE

Someone has recently told me that I was a fool to take my 11-month springer bitch out shooting at the end of the season. Why? She does all that is asked of her and just needs experience which she obviously cannot get sitting at home in the kennel.

Although a dog may appear ready for the real thing at a very early age, there are many potential problems which could arise from being too keen. The most immediate one which springs to mind is that of hard mouth – the sooner the dog appears on the shooting field, the sooner he is likely to retrieve a pricked pheasant and the sooner he is likely to be 'spurred' (see the section on *hard mouth*, p.47).

Also, beginning training at too tender an age may take a lot of natural ability away from the dog and this in turn can make him over-reliant on the handler, rather than on his own instinct. Very basic training, however, such as walking on a lead and teaching your dog to sit to command can be started quite early (around 14 weeks) but no serious training should even be considered before the age of approximately six months for labradors and spaniels, and as late as nine to 12 months for some of the other breeds such as golden and flat-coated retrievers. Much obviously depends upon the breed and temperament of the individual. A bold puppy can begin hand training earlier than a shy one. A patient handler can begin the training of a puppy at quite a tender age, but anyone inclined to impatience should defer training until the pupil is less likely to be nervous of a sudden outburst of temper. (In an ideal world, of course, such an event would never happen.)

If training is not begun before approximately six months, there is no way that a dog can be experienced at the age of 11 months. Remember that it is better to miss one season's shooting with your springer bitch, or any other dog, and have an easily biddable dog for the next ten years or so than to risk taking her out too soon and ruining her. Apart from anything else, there is the financial side to consider; a replacement puppy is an expensive item which can be avoided with a little time, patience and forethought.

You should also consider the possibility that if you persist in taking out an unruly gundog in company, invitations are likely suddenly to 'dry up', or the gamekeeper will never be able to forgive you for the fact that your dog has just run-in and pushed his pheasants back over the heads of the beaters.

Never be tempted into beginning training too early – six months is soon enough for a spaniel.

TRAINERS' TIPS

- Six months is soon enough. You must know the capabilities of an individual and, of course, he must know the kennel/daily routine before any attempt at training is made.

- Better later than sooner.

BOREDOM

When I throw the dummy nowadays, my retriever, who used to be quite keen, seems a bit bored. Also he's started to hesitate before picking up and sometimes he just leaves it. What can I do?

Peter Moxon, writing in one of his excellent articles in *The Shooting Times*, quoted the dictionary definition of boredom: 'making weary by constant repetition'. Professional trainers are far less likely to bore their dogs than are amateurs who, because they only have one, or maybe two, youngsters to train, tend to spend every available spare minute in lengthy, tedious and repetitive lessons. The professional, on the other hand, does not have time to overdo the various exercises with each individual and he quickly learns the art of knowing how far to go and when to stop.

By overdoing dummy lessons, for instance, general boredom is bound to result. Dogs are intelligent animals and need constant stimulation. It is not surprising, therefore, that a dog continually asked to retrieve plain,

falling-within-sight, hand-thrown dummies, rebel. Retrieving can and should be made much more interesting. After all, the only point in having a retriever is to find and collect game which has fallen either out of sight or is otherwise inaccessible.

All of the training manuals advise that once a dog has reached a certain stage of proficiency, finding, picking-up and delivering a simple retrieve should be stopped and the dog should be encouraged to use his nose by seeking the less obvious. To this end, early exercises should include work in increasingly thick cover and eventually end with artificially laid lines of scent leading to a previously concealed retrieve.

'Ringing the changes' with a different type of dummy can sometimes work well but it is far

Never bore a dog with repetitive dummy work.

better not to allow the problem to arise in the first place. Dummies may be made from all kinds of materials ranging from canvas purpose-stitched affairs to an old rabbit skin or an old woollen sock.

The 'real thing' can also cause boredom. Peter Moxon quotes an instance where, 'a quite renowned retriever was sent to collect a dead pigeon over a fence lying quite clearly in the open. He quickly found the bird, slowly walked up to it and . . . cocked his leg . . . The handler turned to the judge in horror and expostulated, "I just can't understand it – I had him out in the woods last night during a pigeon shoot and he must have picked up over thirty birds".'

TRAINERS' TIPS

- Rest the dog completely for a month, taking it out for the minimum of exercise necessary to keep it fit and healthy. (The exercise should be free-running.)

- Train at different venues. Water work is excellent on hot summer days. It is not necessary to train every day. Any retrieving should be done over varying distances and over obstacles.

BREEDING

My German shorthaired pointer bitch is shortly due to come into season and at a recent working test another trainer seemed to be impressed by the way she worked. He suggested that I use his dog and, instead of a stud fee, he would be happy to receive a puppy in due course. What potential problems do I need to consider before going ahead and saying 'yes'?

Firstly, before breeding from any bitch, the sire should be carefully chosen. This is very definitely a case in which the novice owner/trainer/breeder needs to seek some professional advice and find out some of the blood lines associated with both bitch and dog. Most trainers stress that you should not breed from a bitch unless it is for the good of the breed in general and it should be remembered that, in most cases, all but one of the resultant litter will be sold on. In due course, these will be bred from and without care, this could result in a particular inefficiency in the breed.

Beware, as a bitch owner, of a breeder who offers a stud dog in return for the 'pick of the litter'. An experienced owner obviously knows how best to pick a puppy and surely it is in your interest to keep the best for yourself? Far better, therefore, to agree to a set stud price rather than the return of a puppy.

As to the earliest age that you should begin breeding from a bitch, it should certainly not be before the age of 18 months. Some trainers state 'not before the second heat', but as this can be as early as 12 months, this

dictum should not be followed.

Most of the vets whom I contacted in connection with this book suggest that the bitch should be sound and have been checked and passed for hips and eyes where relevant.

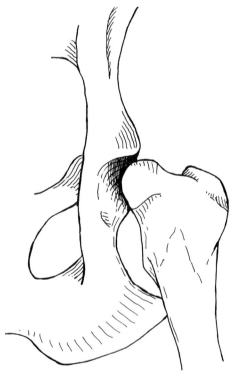

Before breeding, the possibility of hip dysplasia should be considered. As well as carefully scrutinizing the parents' pedigrees, the scores available as a result of testing for the BVA/KC Scheme must be examined. Illustrated here is a moderate case taken from the x-ray of a Labrador.

Spaniels, for instance, tend to suffer from eye and ear problems and they must have an Eye Clearance Certificate before being allowed to enter field trials.

As an owner and trainer of spaniels, I know that ears are an on-going problem. Although unlike their show counterparts, working spaniels have smaller and therefore, less intrusive ears, nevertheless, brambles and barbed wire are likely to cause problems. This factor is not a result of either *breeding* nor *breeding defects* (see following sections).

TRAINERS' TIPS

● Think through the situation. Have I the time? Do I have the facilities for whelping a bitch? Can I sell the puppies to suitable homes?

● It does not harm the bitch in any way if she never has a litter.

Spaniels tend to suffer from eye and ear problems; labradors from hip dysplasia. All should be checked before considering breeding.

BREEDING DEFECTS

According to both the paperwork and the breeder from whom I bought my bitch, she is 'sound'. Are there any defects which would prevent my breeding from her?

It would appear that all gundog breeds are susceptible to one or another of a multitude of possible defects and so, although a bitch may appear sound, you should always make a point of seeking advice from a vet.

Although the parents of a particular animal may, in fact, have certificates claiming that they are free of hip displasia for example, this does not necessarily mean that their offspring are immune to potential problems. If the dog is one of the various retrieving breeds, it is likely that a vet will suggest that he checks both hips and eyes and scores them on the British Veterinary Association/ Kennel Club Scheme.

Spaniels are subject to cataracts and ear problems. Although the latter problem is more likely to be a veterinary one rather than a question of heredity, it is as well to make sure before embarking on a breeding

programme. Other genetic troubles that can be passed on are in-growing eyelashes and either under- or over-shot jaws.

Apart from the medical aspects, you should also consider defects which may already be apparent in the bitch or in her parents: hard mouth, whelping capabilities and an unwillingness to train are just a few problems that spring immediately to mind. (See also *breeding*, p.16.)

TRAINERS' TIPS

- Sam Seall says, 'The list is very long and a whole book could be written on this subject alone. I do not think that most people with one bitch ever consider these problems when they decide that, "it is good for the bitch to have one litter".'

BREEDS

I have a friend who has a litter of cocker spaniel pups for sale and I am very tempted to buy one even though most of my shooting is from a peg, at driven birds. Would a cocker make a good retriever?

Particular breeds are obviously more suited to certain jobs than others. Bearing in mind the fact that, with luck, your eventual choice will be a shooting companion for around ten years, it therefore behoves any potential purchaser to ensure that a dog is bought with a purpose in mind rather than on a mere whim.

Taking the problem illustrated as an example, a cocker would not be the most suitable choice for someone intending only to shoot driven birds. Of all the spaniel breeds, a cocker has, arguably, the most 'get-up and go' and, once sent out at the end of a heavy drive, adrenalin takes over from discipline and he will, quite literally, get up and go! Far better, therefore, for the questioner merely to admire his friend's dogs and choose instead one of the more orthodox retrieving breeds.

Labradors, golden and flat-coated retrievers are the most obvious choices and, provided that they are

Choose a breed which will most suit the type of work expected.

English springer spaniel

Labrador/retriever

German shorthaired pointer

bought from a reputable breeder who uses working animals rather than those bred for show purposes, any potential problems are likely to be lessened.

As an aside, I have, on my own shoot, two beaters who use golden retrievers bred from show rather than working stock and I have to say that they are perfect in the beating line. Perhaps exceptions which disprove the rule? Generally, however, it is better to buy a dog to suit the individual's type of shooting: a retrieving breed for the peg and a spaniel or HPR (Hunt, Point, Retrieve) breed for the rough-shooter.

Cross-breeds, a labrador cross-springer for instance, are very rarely a good purchase. It might be supposed that by cross-breeding the result would prove to be a good all-rounder, but experience proves that you end up with the worst rather than the best of both worlds.

TRAINERS' TIPS

- It's a case of 'horses for courses'. Spaniels do not like sitting at pegs and I do not advise using retrievers for hunting as they usually range too far ahead.

Choosing the right breed is an important factor in avoiding potential problems. Basically, however, it is a choice between either one of the spaniel or retriever breeds or an all-round HPR type.

CHASING

Perhaps naively, I have been under the impression that the instinct to point will always overcome that of chasing. Last Wednesday, however, my German Shorthaired Pointer rushed in at a point and ran riot after a rabbit. Up until then I have always been quite proud of my dog, especially as the rest of my rough-shooting colleagues frequently appear to have problems when their spaniels, and labradors chase anything that gets up.

Although chasing can be a problem with all breeds of gundog, it depends upon the breed and type of work expected of it as to when the problem is likely to occur.

Basically, spaniels and HPRs have more temptation thrust in front of their noses because the nature of their duties means that they are questing for game, occasionally working out of immediate contact with the handler. In such a situation, it is all too easy for a dog to begin to chase a rabbit and when, perhaps because the trainer cannot see the dog, it is not stopped, the chase continues.

Retrieving breeds on the other hand, generally only ever come into contact with unshot game when on their way out to a retrieve and, if the early training is all that it should have been, it is a relatively simple matter for the handler to blow the 'stop' whistle and then redirect his dog. (The importance of whistle training cannot be over-emphasized and I have seen the life of a spaniel spared as it responded immediately to a single blast whilst in pursuit of a wounded cock bird which ran across a busy road.)

The fact that you might be working a dog alongside those less well-trained than your own can also be a hindrance and if an unruly pack hurtles past a dog which hitherto has been obeying his master's commands, perhaps the dog cannot be entirely blamed for wanting to join in the fun. This is another case for choosing your

To prevent a retrieving breed chasing unshot game, you should be able to blow the 'stop' whistle and then redirect the dog.

sporting companions carefully!

Most professional trainers are of the opinion that if and when chasing problems occur it is because early training has not been done correctly, and they subsequently feel that the first rectifying step must be to return to basics. Retrieving breeds developing this problem should immediately embark on a complete steadiness programme without any dummy or other picking-up work being offered.

TRAINERS' TIPS

- If a dog chases on a shooting day then, sadly, the homework has not been done. Back to the rabbit pen and basic training.

- Make sure that the dog is absolutely on the whistle and stops when the whistle is blown. Give the dog a few sessions in a rabbit pen (see p.86). Ensure that the dog is used to cattle, sheep or even the ducks in the park.

- Go back to basics. If all else fails, try using a check cord (see opposite).

CHECK-CORDS

I am just beginning the education of my first gundog. My wife gave me a training book for my birthday and it mentions using a check-cord. How and when to use it is fully explained but it has since occurred to me that (a) without the resources of a rabbit pen, I might be dragging my dog around the countryside for ages before being in the position where it is tempted into chasing and (b) seeing as dogs are so intelligent, surely it will know when it is and when it is not on the check-cord.

A check-cord is merely an extended lead, applied in order to give an animal enough room to be able to hunt and quarter the ground but, at the same time, be under total control. Should an experienced retriever, for example, begin chasing unshot game while on his way out to pick-up, then the handler can take the dog to where he knows there is plenty of ground game. Affix the adapted washing-line, or whatever, around the dog's neck, thereby obtaining both the control and wherewithal to pull back sharply when the dog attempts to either run-in or ignore the 'stop' whistle.

Before using a check cord, you should endeavour to seek out a helpful trainer who can advise as to its correct use. In the wrong hands, it may, in fact, cause more problems than it cures. The line-drawing on this page shows how it should be fixed round the neck so that the cord slackens when the pressure is released and does not choke the dog. (The same method applies when putting on a slip-lead.)

Unfortunately, if used too often a dog does begin to realize when it is on the cord and may well behave perfectly, reverting to its old uncontrollable self when not. (See also *coming to call*, p.24.)

TRAINERS' TIPS

- If the check-cord is hardly ever used but brought out for special training sessions, it works to good effect. If over used, the dog soon becomes aware of cord and reacts accordingly.

- Check-cords should not be used unless the person knows what he is doing.

- A check-cord should only be used as a last resort.

Correct application of either a check-cord or slip-lead is important.

COMING TO CALL OR WHISTLE

There is no definite reason I can think of why my springer has suddenly become reluctant to return to the whistle. Up until recently, even when she would not answer to my voice, she would always run back to me after I gave three toots on my whistle.

Unfortunately, this problem can occur with any gundog breed and it is always useful to remember that the further any dog goes away, the less control the handler has over it. Bearing this fact in mind, make a point of getting to know your own animal and never take your eyes off him during training or exercise. If, whilst out in an open field for instance, he dives off into the edge of a wood, get him back before he either discovers the hidden pleasures therein or realizes that the owner has not the same degree of control in there as he has in an open space.

With correct training the handler should know at what distance his trainee is likely to be less responsive to the whistle and that distance should never be exceeded.

Handlers who, perhaps because of work commitments, are forced to train in the dark have one advantage. Darkness makes a dog less inclined to run away for fear of being left behind. Gamebirds are obviously up at roost and less likely to be a distraction.

Bending down will encourage even an experienced dog to return quickly.

TRAINERS' TIPS

- Blow the whistle or call out before walking or running backwards, making the dog think that he is likely to be left behind.

- Bend down to make bodily presence smaller and therefore more encouraging to approach.

- Go back to general obedience training and prevent your dog from going over too great a distance.

- This problem can be cured by using the check-cord. Allow the dog to run around dragging the check-cord. Every so often call the dog's name or blow the re-call whistle, positioning yourself so that you can pick up the end of the cord and give a quick tug at the same time. This should not be overdone as a dog soon learns when it is on or off the cord. When the dog comes to you, praise him and repeat the exercise.

- If the pup has been used to walking with you at an early age (from eight weeks onwards), this problem does not normally arise. If the problem does arise, run in the opposite direction or crouch down and turn away or show him some item to retrieve. Call and/or whistle at the same time.

COMMANDS

Having just begun my dog's training, I have been borrowing books in the subject from my friends and the local library. One book (talking about retrievers), says that I should tell my dog to 'sit'; another stipulates that I should use 'hup' as a command. I don't want to confuse my dog with too many orders so what do you consider to be the best basic commands?

It doesn't matter which command you use as long as it is the same one each time. If too many commands are given for the same action, the dog, no matter what breed, will become confused and not know what is expected of it. Traditionally, a retriever is told to 'sit' while a spaniel is trained to 'hup' but it matters little whether it is told to 'sit' or 'sausages'

or even 'stand' just so long as the *same* command for the *same* action is always given.

The tone and inflection in the handler's voice should also be consistent. If you tell a dog in a soft tone that it is a 'bad dog', he will probably wag his tail. Tell him that he is a 'good dog' in a gruff voice and his tail will disappear between his legs.

Beware of 'nagging' a dog. There is absolutely no point in telling a dog continuously to 'get on'. Give the command at the beginning of the order and only again if he hesitates and looks back. In this instance the order should also be accompanied by a hand signal (see p.45). All too often you hear handlers, especially those of the hunting breeds, give their particular 'hunt on' command over and over again. All this does is create a constant background noise for the dog which he will quickly learn to ignore.

Keep commands simple. By inserting the dog's name before the command is given, there can be no doubt for whom the instruction is intended.

Remember too that ground conditions will affect the dog's response to a particular command. There have been countless occasions when a hunting breed appears to go

BASIC COMMANDS

Heel
Sit or hup
Leave – to prevent chasing of rabbits, for example
Get on – to cast out, either to hunt or retrieve
Get back – to cast further out, when retrieving
Over – to jump or cross water
One toot or blast on whistle – to stop
Several short toots or blasts – to recall

out of control whilst beating through a piece of kale. The owner shouts, blows his 'stop' whistle – all to no avail. Sometimes the animal is, in fact, being belligerent but, more often than not, it is genuinely not able to hear any orders as it thrashes through the kale leaves. Put yourself in the same position and imagine the noise that these leaves bashing against your ears would make and how it would affect your ability to hear.

As a result of contacting some professional trainers in connection with this book, one of them, Sam Seall, came up with what he considers to be an important point and, as it comes from a successful, experienced handler, it should be given due mention: always say the dog's name first, before giving any commands.

TRAINERS' TIPS

- 'Sit and stay' is not necessary as after being told to sit, a dog should automatically stay until told otherwise. Cut down on unnecessary commands.

- Over the years, I have discovered that the more commands you give to the owners, the more they forget.

- Concentrate on getting the dog 100 per cent on one command before confusing it with another. This is especially important with a timid dog, who may be unsure of himself, and an owner who is likely to lose his temper.

No matter what basic command is given, vocal directives and hand signals must be both *definite* and *consistent*.

CONCENTRATION

We have a very biddable black labrador who, most of the time, responds well to training. I have noticed, however, that should I continue a lesson for too long, concentration seems to go. This worries me greatly as I wonder whether our particular black labrador has the aptitude to be a good gundog.

Any dog will lose concentration and become bored if the training session is carried on for too great a period of time, or if the trainer insists on the same boring exercises day after day.

It is, therefore, far better to do one or two ten-minute sessions rather than one lasting an hour or more.

Too many would-be trainers seem to be frightened that unless their dog undergoes proper discipline as described by the book on a daily basis, all their previous hard work will be forgotten by the pupil. This is not true and a dog will in fact benefit from the odd day's 'holiday'. Exercise must of course still be given and during these periods the 'stop' and 'recall' whistle and heel work will form a natural part of the walk, instilling yet further some of the early basic training.

The degree of concentration required by an individual dog depends to some extent on whether it is being trained as merely a shooting companion or for the more competitive world of field trials. In the latter case, it is generally true to suppose that a higher degree of concentration over a greater period of time is needed in order that the dog be constantly alert and aware of what the handler is asking. This comment is not meant to imply in any way that the general shooting dog need to be any less well-trained, only that a few minor mistakes can be tolerated whereas in a trial they would be penalized by the judges.

TRAINERS' TIPS

- Keep all lessons very short and varied.

- Make training a pleasure for you and the dog. Try and vary the exercises and train on different grounds as much as possible.

DELIVERY

Although my golden retriever picks up well, she will not bring the dummy right up to me. How can I ensure that she makes a classic 'field trial' delivery?

All dogs which are eventually to be used on the shooting field must, no matter what other faults they have, bring their retrieve right up to the handler and hold it firmly but gently until he is ready to accept it. There is an obvious reason for this: no matter how good the shooting has been, there are bound to be wounded birds.

A dog which retrieves a pricked bird to within a yard or two of the handler and then drops it before it has been humanely dispatched is likely to end up retrieving the same bird two or three times as it attempts to make good its escape into the nearest cover. This is embarrassing for the owner, and more importantly, distressing and cruel to the quarry.

Sometimes, this problem will occur after a dog has been retrieving well for some time and if this occurs, the handler must analyse the possible reasons. Very often, a poor delivery

stems from a lack of trust between dog and handler. The dog may, for instance, be 'hand shy' which could have been caused by the trainer snatching at the dummy in earlier lessons.

Retrieves from water may make the dog put down the dummy/bird upon reaching dry land so that he can shake excess water from the coat. Nine times out of ten, once this is done, the dog will pick up the retrieve again and bring it on to his master. If, instead of encouraging the dog to pick-up quickly after shaking, the handler shouts and swears at the dog, then obviously the animal will, in time, become reluctant to continue its journey, thinking that it has done wrong.

Another point to remember, is never to take your eye off the dog once sent out to retrieve and ensure that you are ready and able to take the retrieve immediately the dog returns. This may seem obvious but I have, on many occasions, seen a dog sent out and then the owner begins a business discussion with his neighbouring gun, with the result that the dog is wandering around his owner with a bird clamped in his mouth. Eventually, his jaw begins to ache and, quite naturally, he drops the bird. When the owner realizes that the dog is back and has dropped the bird, a crack across the back with a shooting stick and the words 'bad dog', confirms to the dog that he has been naughty in retrieving the bird, rather than the truth that the handler is, of course, cross that the bird has been dropped.

A generally nervy dog may be reluctant to bring a retrieve to hand because he dislikes eye contact. Where this is thought to be the case, it has been suggested that dummy training should be carried out in the dark so that direct eye contact is avoided.

TRAINERS' TIPS

- If a dog does not hand over or drops his retrieve, walk or run backwards in order to make the dog think that he is going to be left behind. Slap your thighs.

- Stand with your back to a wall or fence so that the dog cannot circle around you. Encourage the dog to lift its head, by giving the command to 'sit' and pat your own chest. Praise the dog *after* you have taken the dummy, *not* before.

- Don't snatch or drag a dummy from your dog.

- If a dog is thought to be hand shy, keep your hands behind your back until he is right up to you.

A classic delivery where the dog is both eager and confident enough to bring the dummy to hand.

DIARRHOEA

After travelling from Surrey to North Yorkshire for the grouse shooting, my springer dog had an attack of diarrhoea and was too miserable to work for the two days I had been invited. Could this problem be one which may prevent my working the dog in future?

Although of a veterinary nature, rather than a training problem, ill health will obviously cause difficulties with working a gundog. Diarrhoea, in particular, can stem from a variety of causes.

In the case of the problem outlined here, it is probable that it was caused by stress brought about by long-distance travelling, a short stay in unaccustomed premises and a break in the feeding routine.

In other cases, however, it can be caused by the wrong diet, bad kennel conditions or worms. If, therefore, your dog seems to be prone to regular bouts of diarrhoea, you should, of course, consult your veterinary surgeon but, before doing so, consider the above and take steps to remedy the situation. There is no point in the vet providing short-term action if, through ignorance, you allow the cause of the problem to continue.

Travelling long distances to the grouse moors, for example, can be one cause of diarrhoea.

TRAINERS' TIPS

- Consider disease as well as the usual possibilities. Consult the vet if symptoms persist.

- Starve your dog overnight, then feed small meals of white meat and rice.

- Find a food that suits the dog, feed it moderately every day and keep the kennel clean at all times.

DIET

When I eventually begin working my large munsterlander on our local rough-shoot, do I need to alter his diet from the all-in-one food I am currently using?

Most trainers and gundog owners with more than one dog in their kennels feed one or another of the many varieties of ready-mixed foods available at any animal feed suppliers. There is much to be said in their favour. First, they are convenient and the mixing of biscuits, meat and gravy is thus avoided. Secondly, they are prepared by professional nutritionists rather than on a hit-and-miss basis, thereby ensuring that protein, oils, fats, fibres and carbohydrates are at the level required for health and stamina. Thirdly, a general feeding guide is usually given.

Remember, however, that it is only a general guide and working dogs may require extra, whilst less active and elderly dogs need less. Most trainers would put a working dog on to a higher protein diet. Bitches feeding puppies can require up to four times their normal daily quantity of food. Whilst there should be no need to change foods as a young dog begins his working career, if – for one reason or another – it is decided to change brands, it is advisable to do so gradually in order to avoid any internal upsets. (See also *worms* p.144, *exercise* p.36, *kennel management* p.57, *diarrhoea* p.31, and *feeding* p.38.)

DIRTY KENNELS

I have, for the first time in my shooting life, bought a bitch puppy; previously I have always had dogs. The problem is, she seems to dirty her kennel more than her male predecessors. I have been told that bitches are dirtier in their kennels than dogs. Is this true?

Once a regular feeding and exercise routine is established, there is no reason why a bitch should be any messier than a dog. Terrier owners who kennel their dogs say that males tend to make more mess than females and often go to the trouble of constructing small, totally enclosed beds rather than the more usual kennel to prevent any unnecessary soiling. Fortunately, gundog breeds do not seem to be as prone to these unwelcome habits but if after a period of time, during which you have followed the 'trainer's tips', the problem persists, then perhaps you should consider a dog bed or 'sky crate'.

Although many professionals feed their dogs in the early evening, I have found that by feeding my dogs at lunch time I very rarely have any problems. They are exercised three times daily: morning, after feeding and last thing at night. By the time the evening walk arrives, waste body matter has passed through and is evacuated on this walk, leaving the dogs empty and comfortable for the night.

Puppies and young dogs cannot, of course, control their bladders and bowels as efficiently as an adult dog but this will come with time. The emphasis in correcting this problem must be put on exercise at *regular*

intervals. (See also *exercise* p.36, *worms* p.144, *kennel management* p.57, and *feeding* p.38.)

TRAINERS' TIPS

- Kennels should always be cleaned when they are dirty, *not* just once a day.

- A good sign in visiting a kennels is the state of cleanliness. If the kennels are dirty, avoid sending your dog there.

- There is no excuse for a dirty kennel.

Young dogs cannot be expected to be as clean in the kennel as would older animals who are well used to a regular feeding and exercise routine.

DROPPING TO COMMAND AND/OR SHOT

All training manuals make much of the need to have a dog proficient at dropping to command and/or shot. Even I, as a novice trainer, can see the need for a dog to drop when commanded by either voice or whistle but I am a little unsure of the need to drop to shot.

I am intending to use my spaniel in the beating line on a shoot where, on average, 300-plus birds are shot every day. Surely, she cannot be expected to drop every time a shot is fired as she would be on her tummy for most of the drive.

Most spaniels used in the beating line do not drop to shot. W H Carlton writing *Spaniels, their Breaking for Sport and Field Trials* in 1915, stated that:

> The only degree of steadiness that is essential is such as will ensure that the dog does not spoil the shot and will not, by retrieving without orders, put up other stuff out of shot or while the gun is unloaded.

The best way to compass this is to break your dog to drop to fur and wing and also to drop to shot.

In working tests, a spaniel is expected to 'drop' both when a bird is flushed and/or when a shot is fired.

After describing the training method, Carlton goes on to say, 'In time he connects the shot with dropping and goes down whenever he hears it . . . see that he drops without hesitation, and does not move until you start him off again.'

It can be seen from the above, therefore, that whereas it is useful to have a dog which will indeed drop to shot when the only shooting that you intend to do is on your own or with a couple of friends over ground on which game is scarce, Carlton's insistence on a dog which drops every time a single shot is fired would not work when beating on a large, well-stocked shoot.

Whilst most professional trainers do not train a retrieving breed to sit upon hearing a shot, it is a different matter when training a spaniel or HPR breed. Presumably, once the lesson has sunk in, it is then up to the owner to decide whether, after considering his own particular type of shooting, he should continue to insist on dropping to shot.

Dropping to command is, however, a very different matter and is a very important exercise which must be thoroughly learned. Once again, provided that the basic hand training has been given correctly, beginning

with the dog close to you, the command 'sit' or 'hup' spoken together with a raised outstretched hand, there should be no problem.

When the animal is proficient at this, the next stage would be to include the whistle and/or shot, gradually extending the distance between you and the dog until you can do it at 100 to 150 yards.

TRAINERS' TIPS

As I began this section by quoting Carlton, I can do no better than include his 'trainer's tip' when experiencing difficulty in getting a dog steady to shot:

. . . do not let him hunt; keep him at heel – as a last resort trailing a check-cord – see that he drops to your shot, and send him retrieving but seldom. Also take him ferreting; drop him by your side, if necessary pegging him down with a check-cord just long enough to enable him to reach the burrows; when the check-cord has spun him once or twice, he ought to cure himself.

EXERCISE

I am really looking forward to my first season's picking-up with my two-year-old labrador. In the summer he became a little overweight despite the fact that I keep a strict eye on his diet. What type of exercising regime do you advise (a) to lose excess weight and (b) to ensure he is fit enough for the coming season?

Although obviously not working, it is still extremely important to keep all breeds of gundogs reasonably fit during the summer months but, in cases where dogs are kept kennelled together, great care must be taken to ensure that they are not so fit as to make them on edge and more inclined to squabble as a consequence.

The form that exercise takes varies from kennel to kennel but as a general rule you should be aiming to cover around three to four miles a day during the close season. The average walking speed of a human being is around three to four miles an hour. You might reasonably assume that an hour's exercise is all that is required, but in actual fact it is far better to break this into three separate and therefore shorter periods spread evenly throughout the day. By doing

so, the dogs are less inclined to become bored through long spells in kennel confinement and will also keep their kennels cleaner.

Summer exercise is a good time to introduce water work (see p.131) and once they are used to water, you will notice that gundogs derive as much enjoyment from splashing about on a sunny day as do children.

If time allows, the three exercise periods should be exclusive of training time but it is unlikely that the average working owner will have enough time in the day. (I do, however, know of several, 'one-dog' owners who take their dogs to work with them in order that they can put in a little training during the lunch-break. But remember, never leave a dog in the confines of a car during the hot summer months.)

Ideally each exercise period should last around half an hour but, no matter what the time allocated, the trainer should try and make these periods as beneficial as possible to the mind of his dog, as well as to his body. Exercise on the road has many advantages, not least of which is keeping pads hard and claws in good condition. Heel work can be practised and it will, of course, help in the education of young dogs as they come across cars, people and bicycles.

As the summer progresses, some form of more strenuous exercise may be required before the shooting season commences. There is no doubt that regular exercise throughout the summer entails less wear and tear on your dog than if he were allowed to get really 'soft' and out of condition and then have to undergo a sudden period of very intensive and strenuous fitness training.

If, no matter how long you exercise one dog, it still seems incapable of a day's work and remains overweight, cut down or change the food until the required balance is achieved. As Sam Seall remarked, 'All the exercise in the world will not run the fat off a dog. It has to be done by diet and with the correct amount and type of food.' Also, Richard Webb warns, 'chronic hip dysplasia will cause a dog to be incapable of a day's work'.

Exercise periods are a good time to let dogs relax and explore their surroundings.

TRAINERS' TIPS

- I take six or eight dogs into a large field or area which is free of game or any livestock and allow them complete free running with no whistle or commands. The only time I use a whistle is to re-call them to take them back to their kennels.

- This, in addition to a sensible diet, enables our dogs to do three or four days a week picking-up and still have a bit of 'go' at the end of the day.

- In the summer I try to give them water work as often as possible. This exercise certainly gets them fit and I would strongly recommend it.

Summer months can be used to introduce them to water in whatever way is available.

FALSE POINTING

As a result of reading various books and magazines, I believe that my young dog is guilty of what is known as 'false pointing'. Can this be rectified?

False pointing is generally only a problem with either pointers, setters or the HPR types. Most, if not all, of these breeds will be worked on the small rough-shoot or walking-up grouse when it can be somewhat embarrassing to handle a dog which continually 'tells lies'. This is when the dog stands on point where game has been rather than in cover which actually contains game at the present moment.

Most young gundogs of whatever breed are guilty of false pointing at some stage during their early training and the fault is due mainly to a lack of experience. This usually resolves itself as and when the dog gains experience of all types of game and learns to differentiate between an old lingering scent and a good positive find.

TRAINERS' TIPS

- A dog that continues to false point should be given plenty of work on game.

FEEDING

Can incorrect feeding be the cause of any problems during early training?

Although in itself bad or incorrect feeding cannot really be an excuse for any problems which may occur during training nor, in fact, during subsequent working, a correctly fed dog is a happy one and is therefore more inclined to respond favourably to either training or work. However, an unbalanced diet can cause a dog to be overactive thus causing training problems.

Overfeeding will, however, obviously result in an obese and lethargic animal which, because of being overweight, will be reluctant to work efficiently and energetically.

Most professional trainers have, over the past decade or so, gone over to one of the many 'all-in-one' dog foods so readily obtainable from most animal feed suppliers. There are several reasons for this, perhaps the first of which is convenience. In establishments where there are more than a couple of gundogs it is obviously easier to scoop out the required amounts of manufacturer-prepared food from a bag or bin and carry out the bowls to the kennels rather than have to mess about opening tins, boiling water or mixing porridge and adding cereal.

Not only can this type of food go off and as a result lead to digestive problems, but the purchase of several meats and various meals is, as a general rule, more expensive, and the preparation is more time-consuming.

Perhaps most importantly, when you mix your own food, there is no absolute certainty that it is being given to the dog at the correct nutritional level nor that proteins and other constituents are sufficient for the health of a working animal.

TRAINERS' TIPS

- The choice of food is a matter of personal decision and provided that it is fresh and uncontaminated, there should be no problem.

- Feed times should be chosen to coincide with a time when it is known that, barring unforeseen circumstances, someone will be there to prepare and give the meal. Dinner is such an important part of an animal's routine that difficulties are bound to arise if food is given at 10.00am one day and 10.00pm the next.

- Find a food that suits the dog and your pocket best.

- All of our dogs are fed on an all-in-one feed and we are very pleased with their condition. If you have puppies look out for the special all-in-one puppy foods.

- An ideal diet would be raw tripe and biscuit but it can be difficult to get a good supply of tripe, which should be unbleached.

Provided that the correct type of all-in-one food is purchased and that the manufacturer's recommendations normally found on the bag are adhered to, this is one potential worry alleviated.

Remember too to experiment and find a food which suits the dog, as a food which is high in meat may not suit a delicate digestive system as well as one which contains a higher level of cereal. However, never change a dog's food overnight and if, for whatever reason, it is thought necessary to 'ring the changes', first add a little of the proposed new food to the animal's present diet, gradually increasing the amount daily. (See also *exercise p.36, worms p.144, and kennel management p.57.*)

FIELD TRIALS

My young spaniel, (now 18 months) has trained up very well and I would like to try him in a working test or even field trial. How do I go about getting a run?

The apparent 'closed shop' world of tests and trials can be a problem to the novice trainer. Advice on this matter from a professional will probably help but a very positive move would be to join a gundog club, the names and addresses of which are held by the Kennel Club.

By joining such an organization, you are entitled to enter the club's trials and you may be given some preference in a trial draw as a result of being a club member. Trials are organized centrally and, although most clubs accept members nationally, they tend to concentrate on one particular geographical area. By being a member, there is a greater chance of obtaining a run and perhaps, more importantly, very often

Working tests are a good introduction to the world of field trialing.

at a member's reduced rate of entry.

Clubs which include summer training sessions tend, as a matter of course, also to run tests and will often set small tests within an ordinary training period in order that handlers can evaluate the progress or otherwise of their own particular prodigy. This undoubtedly helps in planning a dog's future training and subsequent progression. The owner can better decide whether he and the dog are up to the standard required in more competitive meetings.

FIGHTING

Although purchased to accompany me on pigeon-shooting forays, I have been taking my black labrador dog beating on our nearby shoot where he performs well and is, according to the keeper, an asset in the line. Unfortunately, to my embarrassment and to others' annoyance, he just cannot be prevented from fighting with the shoot owner's yellow labrador dog if and when they meet between drives.

It is not unknown for a dog of any particular breed whether gundog or not, to take a dislike to another individual. In most cases, the reason this occurs can be traced to an incident where the aggressor has, at some time in its past, been attacked by a dog of the colour, type, size or temperament which he is now aggressive towards.

Having said this, the gregarious nature of shooting means that people and dogs are working in close contact and are therefore, bound to meet up at the end of a drive, in the back of

the beater's trailer or when kennelled at lunchtime. All gundogs must, for these various reasons, be of a sociable nature and a dog which is an habitual fighter should not, no matter how good he is in other spheres, be taken on a shoot.

The problem usually (but not always) stems from the fact that the dog is more dominant than the owner and is either badly or completely untrained.

There are several ways of avoiding potential problems with regard to fighting and the first and perhaps

On a shooting day (or even at a Field Trial) gundogs are bound to come into contact with each other. Any tendency toward aggression must, therefore, be immediately 'nipped in the bud'.

other and renew old friendships, and a dog which is too keen and is, as a result, seen to be a threat by another, may well be set upon. It has to be far better to follow the professional's advice and keep the dogs in the car until everyone is ready to move off. When they are eventually released, call them immediately to heel so that they cannot mix with the other dogs.

Finally it could be well worth pointing out a theory held by Ron Seale. He believes that a placid and therefore, ideal temperament has been forfeited by some gundog breeders in the rush to improve hereditary problems such as hip dysplasia.

most obvious, is to keep your dog on a lead unless he is actually working. Contrary to popular opinion, a dog on a lead does not mean that he is ill-trained or disobedient and, on the plus side, means that the owner is free to socialize without having to keep a constant eye on his charge.

As a keeper, I see so many instances where, upon arrival at the meeting-place beaters and indeed, guns, let their dogs out to 'empty' themselves whilst the handlers don leggings, check cartridge bags and assemble guns. This is completely unnecessary and the dogs should have had a chance to relieve themselves before leaving home or, if travelling a long distance, at some suitable point *en route*.

Naturally, excited dogs milling around the car park tend to sniff each

TRAINERS' TIPS

● If the dog fights at home, he will obviously have to be kennelled separately. Consider why he might be jealous of other dogs and if possible, take steps to remedy the situation.

● Try corrective training, through chastising immediately.

● Castration can be used in some cases and is usually effective.

G

GUN-SHYNESS/GUN-NERVOUSNESS

As a novice trainer I am interested in the constant references to gun-shy and gun-nervy dogs. Are these two different names for the same problem?

There is a world of difference between a dog which is gun-shy and one which is nervous of the gun. In the former case, shyness is usually hereditary and in the eyes of most professionals cannot be cured or, if it can, is a very long process which should only be tried by an expert. Nervousness, on the other hand, is caused by bad handling and not giving the dog the chance to become accustomed to the sound of a gun firing over a period of time or distance.

It has been suggested that puppies should be acclimatized to sudden noise from a very early age and the best time to do this would appear to be at feed times when the dog's mind

Well before entering the shooting world, young dogs should be accustomed to the sound of gun shot. Start early in training in order to avoid the possibility of a gun-nervy animal.

is otherwise occupied.

A metal dustbin lid makes a good, hollow sound but it should not, of course, be first banged over the head of the eating puppy. Feed the dog in the kennel and go to the farthest point of the garden before testing the reaction. If the noise does not appear to disturb him, move in a little closer and then start at that point the following day.

If space and neighbours permit the use of a small-bore shotgun this can be a more authentic alternative but never be tempted to use a starting pistol or dummy launcher, as the sound given off by these is more of a 'crack' than a 'bang'.

Beware too of noisy children who may, by use of cap-pistols and the like, unintentionally make a young dog nervous.

TRAINERS' TIPS

- Give the dog tit-bits, have an older dog as company and fire a shotgun at long distances, but not in an enclosed area.

- Stand back about 100 yards at a clay-pigeon shoot. Throw dummies at the same time so as to occupy the dog's mind. Alternatively, sit the dog down, stand 30 yards away, fire the gun and then throw the dummy.

HAND SIGNALS

After visiting a field trial as a spectator, I am just beginning to realize the importance of hand signals. What do you consider to be the minimum number of hand signals I should use when I begin training my Welsh springer spaniel and how can I avoid any problems which may arise from confusion? There is, after all, a lot to cope with, including oral commands, whistles and now hand movements.

Heel	–	Necessitates a hand signal either pointing to the handler's left heel or the palm of the hand outstretched from the left hand held straight to the body.	**Get on**	–	Swing arm in required direction.
			Get back	–	Outstretched arm with flat of hand 'pushing' dog away. Repeated action.
			Over	–	Point to obstacle.
Sit or Hup	–	Raised hand showing palm.	**Stay**	–	Same as for 'sit' or 'hup'.

All hand signals must be clear and definite, leaving the pupil in no doubt as to what is required.

On the subject of hand signals all professional handlers and trainers are unanimous in their opinion. If a dog has been trained and schooled correctly there should be no problem with either ignoring hand signals or becoming confused by them.

The signals used must, however, be definite and easily seen by the dog. Sloppy half-movements can easily be misread or even missed totally over a distance of several yards, and so you must first overcome any inhibitions about acting like a demented windmill to the casual observer!

On page 26 I have included a list of basic commands and although most trainers use only three hand signals to accompany these commands, namely 'left', 'right', and 'back', I nevertheless feel it important that you should be aware of all the combinations even if only to understand those given by the professionals whom you might see demonstrating their skills at the Game Fair or similar events.

The recall whistle should be accompanied by the slapping of the thigh. In addition, a dog may be encouraged to range or hunt to right or left by first blowing the 'stop' whistle and then either swinging the right arm to the right or the left arm to the left.

TRAINERS' TIPS

● I use only three: left, right and back. Most novice trainers seem to skip this exercise and hope for the best.

● If the training is done correctly and *in the right order*, then this problem should not arise.

● If a dog ignores your hand signals, as with most problems, it will be necessary to return to basics.

HARD MOUTH

Last Saturday, when picking a bird on our rough-shoot, my GSP ripped the skin from the back of a hen pheasant. On closer inspection, the point where the rib cage attaches to the vertebrae was crushed. I am worried that she has become hard-mouthed. What can I do?

When the question of suspected hard mouth is being discussed, there are many points to consider and the animal in question should always be given the benefit of the doubt.

In the days of dog 'breakers', rather than today's supposedly enlightened trainers, it was accepted that there was no cure for hard mouth.

A one-off case of hard mouth may have several causes. First of all, consider these possibilities: Was the retrieve collected from thick cover? Was it late in the day and was the dog tired? Has the dog been 'spurred' previously – from a running cock for example? Is the dog in question old?

If you are at the field-trial stage, suspected hard mouth is sufficient to eliminate a dog from a particular stake.

Defining hard mouth is not always a simple matter. There are many cases of shot and retrieved game being examined by judges who could not, in their heart of hearts, determine whether or not the damage had been caused by the fall, the shot or the retrieve.

It is absolutely useless, when examining game for damage, to trust eyesight alone as real hard mouth can only be detected by feel. A hard-mouthed dog usually crushes the back and/or ribs and the best way of ascertaining this is to hold the bird by the neck with one hand whilst placing the other under the wings from the back with the thumb in one side and four fingers on the other. It should be possible to feel the ribs. If these are obviously crushed then, unfortunately, you have a genuine case of hard mouth.

Checking a bird for signs of hard mouth.

The definition for detecting hard mouth given by the Kennel Club is as follows:

> A hard mouthed dog seldom gives visible evidence of hardness. He will simply crush in one or both sides of the ribs. Blowing up the feathers will not disclose the damage.
>
> Place the game on the palm of the hand, breast upwards, head forward, and feel the ribs with finger and thumb. They should be sound and firm. If they are caved in or flat, this is evidence of hard mouth.

Although all trainers accept that there is no cure for genuine hard mouth, it still pays to consider the possible reasons why it occurs as, if caused by human error, a future re-occurence may be avoided.

As mentioned earlier but without much explanation, some dogs have become hard-mouthed because they were introduced to live, wounded game either too early or incorrectly and, as a result, were 'spurred' by a lively cock pheasant. A dog will soon learn that if it grips a little tighter, the struggles will cease. Reprimands on a return of retrieve can also lead to problems, as can 'tug-of-war' games among puppies.

Hard mouth can be hereditary and for this reason hard-mouthed dogs should not be bred from. Dedicated breeders have, to a very great extent, bred out the fault but there is always the danger that some unscrupulous breeders, out for a 'fast buck', care little for the finer points.

TRAINERS' TIPS

- Dogs should not be introduced to wounded game until they are competent on dead game.

- I have been able to correct this problem in the past but I was able to nip it in the bud. By and large, there is no recognized cure.

HEALTH

Have you and/or the professional trainers any comments to make on the subject of health in general?

Obviously an alert, bright and healthy dog will respond better to work and training than one which is 'under the weather'.

Some specific aspects of health care are outlined under the relevent sections of this book but as to general health care, two of the professionals make these comments.

TRAINERS' TIPS

- If a dog is correctly fed and exercised, health problems will be kept to a minimum.

- Worm your dog at regular intervals (see *worms*, p.144) and look out for worms in the faeces.

- Your dog should be bathed occasionally to keep his coat free from fleas and lice which can upset the general health of the dog (see *lice*, p.61). Also check the coat for skin disease and other problems.

- Check ears, eyes and nails regularly.

- A good marrow bone now and again will help keep the teeth clean and free from tartar, which can build up especially if you use an all-in-one feed.

HEELWORK

No matter how hard I try, I cannot prevent my cocker spaniel from hunting when walking at heel. Although at the moment I am concentrating hard on not letting her be distracted by the various scents, I know that the moment my attention lapses she will go careering off.

Having got a young dog quartering well, you have to be careful that any attempts to curtail hunting at heel are not at the expense of enthusiasm. Heelwork is, however, a very important factor in gundog training and general obedience, so you must ensure that the basic early training is correctly given.

A gundog should be kept at heel unless actually working. Although normally trained to walk at heel on the handler's left side, a left-handed gun will often train his dog to walk on the right as can be seen here.

TRAINERS' TIPS

- This can be rectified by placing a slip-lead on the dog. Give the command 'heel', at the same time giving a sharp tug on the lead and walking forward. Turn right after a few yards and repeat so that you are walking in a square with the dog on the outside. (Left side for a right-handed trainer, or vice versa.)

After a while the lesson can be repeated but this time turn left with the dog on the inside. After several sessions, repeat this exercise with the lead dragging on the ground until eventually, the lead can be dispensed with totally.

HUNTING

My labrador is very obedient, some would say too obedient! The problem is she will not hunt. She is still very young (18 months). Can this be rectified?

In nine cases out of ten this problem is brought about by over-handling and the dog becoming totally reliant on commands given by the handler. Occasionally, the problem can also originate from over-zealousness in giving too many seen retrieves.

Too much handling at too early a stage in training could mean that the dog has never had the opportunity to use his natural instincts when a puppy and has, to all intents and purposes, become 'over-disciplined'.

The problem can affect all breeds of gundog but it is to be found mainly in the retrieving breeds. Fortunately, the problem can be quite easily rectified.

TRAINERS' TIPS

- Let the dog see you drop a dummy in cover. Walk the dog on for about 30 yards at heel, and then send her back for the dummy. Eventually, you can increase this to 150 to 200 yards. On some occasions put a dummy down without the dog seeing it, walk on as before and send her back. She will soon learn to use her nose.

- Allow the dog to run free where there is likely to be game scent, at all times keeping a check on her.

- This could be the result of boredom in training. Make training situation more like the real thing.

I

INSURANCE

My spaniel, upon being let out of the kennel, ran out into the nearby road and narrowly missed being hit by a car. If she had gone under the wheels and caused an accident, who would have been at fault, me or the car driver?

Any person involved in field sport should be insured. It matters little as to what the chosen sport is. When hunting, your horse can kick or be kicked – it can even be startled and land on a bystander's car bonnet causing a great deal of damage. Fishing and shooting are not without their potential hazards. Unfortunately, not many of us bother to insure our dogs until a vet's bill lands on the doorstep.

TRAINERS' TIPS

● Sam Seall had much to say:

'It is a very good idea to have a trained gundog insured. I heard recently of a spaniel that was shot on a local rough-shoot and the owner is claiming on insurance. I also heard of a dog escaping from its kennel and subsequently being killed by a car. Again this dog was insured and the claim was successful.'

● Most insurance companies, however, put a limit on the value of a dog that is far below its true value.

● It is possible to obtain a 'block' insurance for several dogs. Remember that to replace a trained dog can be expensive.

JUMPING

My springer bitch is, to my mind at least, progressing well. She does, however, have one small problem. Unlike her dam, she will not jump obstacles and despite having mum to 'show her the way', refuses to attempt even the low stone wall which surrounds the garden.

In my personal opinion it is far better to own a dog which is careful about jumping than one which is so head-strong that it will attempt the most unsuitable of obstacles. At the very least it shows that the animal in question is capable of thought and I can best illustrate this by using an example learned long ago by the coursing fraternity.

Although a whippet or greyhound is a fast and efficient means of obtaining a rabbit or hare, individuals of those breeds appear to have very little reasoning power and once the quarry has been sighted, they will course by eye, irrespective of any hedge or barbed wire fence in their way. Obviously this results in numerous trips to the vets. Lurchers, on the other hand, are more careful and this can only be put down to the fact that they have been cross-bred with notably intelligent breeds such as collies.

A sensible dog of any breed is therefore an assset but it can be embarrassing for a handler, competing at a working test for example, to see his dog leap a wire netting fence cleanly and athletically on the outward trip only to fail on the return because the dog is unsure of crossing the self-same obstacle with a dummy in its mouth.

No matter how keen your gundog is, any serious jumping should be avoided before the dog is mature as there is always the risk of possible long-term damage to young bones.

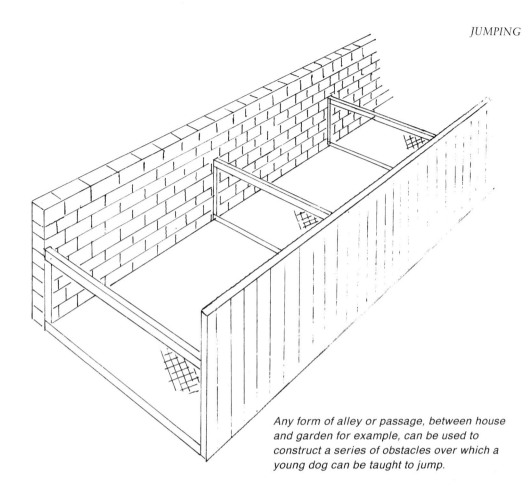

Any form of alley or passage, between house and garden for example, can be used to construct a series of obstacles over which a young dog can be taught to jump.

TRAINERS' TIPS

- I have a small square fenced off at varying heights from 18 inches to three feet. I encourage the dogs to jump in and out of this run.

- A dog can also be encouraged by getting over first yourself and calling the dog to you. If this does not work, put the lead on the dog and gently guide him over the jump at the lowest point.

- Build a jump in an alley-way so that the dog can't run round it. Build up height gradually.

- Place feed in the kennel with a small jump in the doorway so the dog has to jump in to get to his bowl. Alternatively, put the dog in a small area and walk away. Leave an older, more experienced dog with the trainee and call both together. Gradually increase the height of jump.

JUMPING UP

Our Welsh springer lives in the house. He knows not to sit on the furniture but unfortunately he has not yet learnt not to jump up at any visitors. There is no problem in the summer when he is clean and dry but it is a different matter during the winter months when, after a walk, he is wet and muddy.

Professional trainer Sam Seall has a slightly different approach from the norm to this problem. Unlike other trainers, he encourages new trainees and young dogs to jump up for praise. He believes this helps to form a good friendly bond between dog and trainer. However, the dogs have to learn when they are allowed to jump up and when this behaviour is not permitted. A sharp 'no' and a knee in the dog's chest will soon teach him.

My latest addition to the kennel is a cocker spaniel bitch. She is keen and eager to please, and loves affection. Being the size she is, she does not cause me any problem if she jumps up. However, I am sure I would not want to encourage her affection were she a labrador.

Another professional trainer, Richard Webb, seems to agree with me on this point.

TRAINERS' TIPS
● An unpleasant habit and at all costs discourage the dog from jumping up. Beware of losing the dogs confidence, however, when he is returning with a retrieve.
● Push down, at the same time putting your knee in the dog's chest.

A sharp 'no' and a knee in the chest will deter an over-enthusiastic dog from jumping up.

KENNELS

I am shortly to take delivery of my first gundog puppy. We have young children who love animals. Should the puppy be kept in the house or should I make a kennel? I am inclining towards the latter as I don't think it will help training if my children start throwing balls and other things for the dog to play with. My wife thinks a kennel is cruel and that the puppy should be a house dog.

There are two very different schools of thought which become evident whenever the question of kennelling is raised amongst a group of gundog owners. The majority feeling seems to be that a working dog kept in the house is likely to be too 'soft' to be of any use as a sporting companion. It is all too easy for members of the family unwittingly to ruin an animal through lax discipline. Telling a spaniel to 'hup' and not bothering to make sure that the command is carried out, brings it a stage closer to running-in when on the shooting field. Letting a labrador carry a child's doll around the house and then, because no one is around to take the 'retrieve', begin to chew it, is asking for a dog to become hard-mouthed.

On the other hand, by being kept as a house dog, the puppy will all the more quickly become 'humanized' and accustomed to the banging of saucepan lids and the general hurly-burly of domestic life.

With puppies, it is important not to keep them in the kennel for long periods during their first few formative months as, due to a lack of necessary mental stimulation, they will be much slower to mature than ones which have access to continual human contact.

Conversely, if the pup is given too much freedom there may eventually come a time when he gives the owner a complete lack of response, a problem which hardly ever occurs with a kennel-kept dog. Each time the kennel-kept gundog is taken out, his attention will be on the owner and perhaps more importantly, the owner's attention will be on the dog, thereby ensuring that he gets away with nothing.

Perhaps the ideal would be to have a kennel/house dog. Dogs seem to like a routine and it is an undoubted fact that they are upset by the early morning comings and goings of domestic life in the kitchen. When there is breakfast to be made; children to be encouraged into school clothes, fires to be lit, together with all the other chores necessary to begin the day, he would be much happier with a place of his own.

A kennel can also be put to good use when the family is likely to be out for a long period of time and at the very least, may well prevent household furniture from being chewed through boredom and a lack of human contact. One further point worthy of consideration is what should happen when the family go on holiday and it is necessary to make alternative arrangements for your dog.

If a shooting companion or dog-minded friend lives close by, then the dog could be left in his own kennel provided that the person left in charge fully understands his responsibilities and is not going to greet you on your return with the comment, 'Oh yes, Rover had a great time when I took him out; several times he nearly caught a rabbit in the woods'!

Kennels should be well constructed, shaded and yet sunny.

Failing to enlist the help of a reliable friend, you are left with no alternative but to leave the dog in boarding kennels. It is to be strongly recommended that the establishment chosen is one which specializes in gundogs. Instances where kennel maids have had great fun in throwing a ball for the dog to retrieve have been known and this will, of course, soon lead to a dog running-in.

KENNEL CONSTRUCTION AND MANAGEMENT

Are there any problems likely to occur as a result of, or associated with, keeping a gundog kennelled?

Not really. The term kennel management is, after all, merely an umbrella-heading for the various topics concerning health and general well-being covered elsewhere in this book. Worming, feeding and exercise, for example, are all part of the daily kennel routine and are discussed at length in the relevant sections.

Some general guidance on the construction and positioning of the kennel may, however, prevent health problems occurring later in the dog's life.

Provided that they are not allowed to lie in front of the fire one minute and then are put into a kennel in sub-zero temperatures, dogs can endure almost any degree of cold, as long as it is not accompanied by draughts. It is therefore essential that the kennel area be protected from wind which will find its way through cracks in the door, and the dog must not be left

TRAINERS' TIPS

Suggested daily kennel management:

- Exercise morning and night. If it is possible, feed your animals at lunchtime and give them a quick run.

- After the morning walk, the run should be swilled out with the contents of the water bowls and fresh water given.

For a more thorough swilling out, a good-quality disinfectant will remove any stains caused by urine or faeces.

- Bedding can be changed on a weekly rather than daily basis provided that it is not soiled, but the occupants will certainly appreciate the shaking up of whatever material is being used.

facing a wind-tunnel effect every time he enters his run. If there is no alternative location, a kennel which has to be built in an exposed area could be protected by the addition of baffle-boarding or a sheet of corrugated tin around the base. If it is felt necessary to carry out this operation, make sure that the inclusion of some form of wind protection is not to the exclusion of another important factor; namely that the dog's view of its immediate environment is not obscured.

Too much sun brings the danger of both kennel and run turning into an oven during the hottest of weather;

too little leaves the possibility that the dog will be missing out on some of the advantageous vitamins available from the sun's rays. The problems of too much sun can be overcome to some extent by the addition of a tarpaulin sheet fixed over the top of the run. Another answer would be to include a bench in the run area at a height suitable to give the dog the option of sleeping either on top or underneath where it will obviously be a few degrees cooler in the heat of the day.

Drainage is also important and the inevitable water from cleaning out should be able to run off and soak away at a fair distance from the kennel area. Without proper planning, the front of the kennels will soon become an unpleasant quagmire.

Unless used as a sleeping box within an enclosed compound, this type of kennel is not to be recommended. Under no circumstances should any dog be chained to a house of this nature, it being all too easy for the animal to jump over the roof and strangle himself.

LAZINESS

I have been given a show-bred Welsh springer, as its owners are emigrating, and am attempting to train it to the gun. Whilst obedient, it seems to lack the style and drive which I have noticed in other breeds of spaniel working on the shoot. Is there such a thing as laziness in gundogs, does it affect all breeds and is there a remedy?

Some dogs no matter what breed or how good their bloodline, are naturally lazy and will never make good workers.

Bad kennel management, specifically overfeeding which can lead to obesity and/or a boring training routine are other important factors to consider when faced with this problem.

Another cause is trying to train the wrong material. A dog that is predominantly show-bred may have little or no idea nor enthusiasm as to what exactly is required of him.

TRAINERS' TIPS

- There is no real remedy to this problem unless it is merely one of obesity and/or boring training methods. A diet and a rest from training with plenty of free-running exercise would then help.

- Buy a dog initially from good working stock with plenty of field trial champions in the pedigree.

- Never attempt to use a show dog as a worker. It is very rarely worth the effort, although I do know of one or two labradors that have proved to be the exception to the rule.

LESSONS

Only having one dog (a flatcoat), I tend to combine training and exercise. Generally I work him with dummies, both in sight and hidden for about half an hour and then give him some free time for a further ten minutes. Should I increase the length of lessons as I hope to use him picking-up this season?

Although the ideal length of lesson will vary with each individual, they should be kept short and varied. Each task that is asked of the dog should be well within its capabilities and repetitive work with dummies for instance, is bound to become boring no matter how great the intial enthusiasm.

As a general rule 15 to 20 minutes each day is long enough, as over-long lessons on any one particular item almost invariably end with both dog and handler becoming exasperated. This could result in the latter losing his temper and doing something which he later regrets.

The degree of difficulty attached to each task should be increased as quickly as possible so as to add variety, but this should only be done when the handler is absolutely sure that he has instilled the basics. If the dog is one which is normally eager to please and the progression has left him obviously unsure as to what is expected of him, return immediately to an exercise which you know he understands. Never terminate a lesson on a bad note, either with a loss of temper or a task unfulfilled.

There can be no set number of weeks and hours taken to arrive at a certain stage and so how early and how quickly the dog is given these advanced exercises will depend upon the progress of the pupil.

All animals appreciate a routine and will soon be aware of training and feeding times. It is not fair, therefore, to train at 9.00am and for three-quarters of an hour one day and then at lunch-time for five minutes the next. (See also *boredom*, p.14).

TRAINERS' TIPS

- If problems occur with lessons, sometimes a complete rest for a few days helps. When re-commencing, remember to vary exercises to maintain the interest.

- Always give the dog's name before giving any command.

- I do all basic training and heel work in a paddock, graduating to fields and woods as the dog gains experience.

- It does no harm if training is not done every day. Even a dog likes a rest!

LICE

My dog is kennelled underneath our bedroom window and for some time now, we have been woken by the sound of frantic scratching from within the kennel. Has the inhabitant got inhabitants of her own?

Lice are quite common during the warm weather as, unfortunately, are fleas, ticks and mange mites.

An infestation of lice can often be noticed by a dull scaly coat, (not unlike dandruff in humans) and they can sometimes be seen moving in the coat. They are white or yellowish in colour and are roughly the size of a pinhead.

Once the 'itch-scratch' cycle has begun it can be very difficult to prevent the dog from scratching even though the actual cause of the problem has been treated. Injections of cortisone or antihistamines may prove to be the only effective way of breaking this cycle.

Some dogs may scratch, leading the owner to assume that there is some kind of infestation. Occasionally though they may be suffering from skin allergies, the reaction to which is similar to flea and lice attacks (see *skin irritations*, p.100).

Allergic reactions take the form of raised weals on the skin which are small at first but may enlarge rapidly. Dogs which are kept on straw bedding may suffer and it will be necessary to change the type of bedding before the allergy will clear. (Shredded paper is an excellent material, being highly absorbent, dust free and clean.)

Once again, antihistamine injections can help resolve the problem but it should be remembered that dogs can be allergic to penicillin and other antibiotics in the same way as human beings.

VETERINARY TIPS

● There are special insecticidal shampoos and louse powders available. These are very effective in eliminating the lice but, in severe cases, it can take some time thereafter for the hair to grow.

LONGEVITY

How will I know when it is time to have my old gundog put down?

It is often very difficult for any dog owner to decide when is the best time to put down a dog that has been a good and faithful servant. Unfortunately, old dogs seldom die suddenly. More often they gradually decline and this slow deterioration can be unnoticed by the handler and his family due to their day-to-day contact with the animal.

The main problems likely to affect old gundogs are arthritis (often brought about as a result of sitting for hours on a wet salt marsh or picking-up ducks on the last drive or a shooting day and then having to sit for hours in the back of a car or van whilst the owner is in with the host or gamekeeper), muscle stiffness, and difficulty in maintaining body condition.

Growths, both external and internal, often turn out to be cancerous in the older dog and left unattended, will obviously grow to larger and uncomfortable proportions. Dental and ear problems are also more common in old age, although problems with the latter can beset the spaniel breeds at any age.

Because of the difficulty of making a detached judgement, it is very helpful to ask someone else's opinion on this subject. It is often easier for someone else, who does not see the dog every day, to gauge the animal's deterioration and make an objective assessment of its general health and well-being. In theory, this person ought to be your veterinary surgeon but do remember vets are not infallible, and you might like to ask for a second opinion.

TRAINERS' TIPS

- You know your dog best. If he is obviously suffering and is of an age, insist that he is put down. There is little kindness in keeping an old dog alive if it is becoming very weak and thin or is in permanent pain from arthritis.

- Retirement should, wherever possible, be active. A dog that is no longer able to withstand the rigours of a shooting day will still enjoy being taken for the occasional walk.

MARKING

Is there any way in which I can improve the marking ability of my yellow labrador?

The term 'marking' is used by the gundog world to describe the action of watching a dummy or bird fall and having the ability to go straight to it with a fair degree of accuracy.

A dog which has been well schooled in the basics will, by the time he begins dummy work, be well used to watching the trainer's hands and as a result, follow the hand movement when the first dummy is thrown. His eye will take in the dummy as it leaves the hand and follow the parabola to the point where the intended retrieve reaches the ground. It is in this way that a dog first learns to mark.

Some dogs are naturally good markers, others only improve by experience. It is, however, foolish to bore the dog with retrieving lessons in the hope that he will improve his marking ability. This approach is far more likely to develop other problems associated with boredom than it is to heighten the dog's awareness.

TRAINERS' TIPS

- A tip for the handler rather than the dog! If when picking up, you are able to mark the bird and take the dog to the vicinity of the fall, remember that even though you may have marked the bird to be in line with a certain fence post, tree or other land-mark, the fall is never as far out as one might at first suppose.

MATING

I am considering mating my bitch when she next comes into season. How do I know which is the right day to take her to the stud-dog?

A bitch usually comes into season twice yearly and it is generally reckoned that you should not breed from her until the second season at the earliest (see *breeding*, p.16). This gives you ample opportunity to mark down the expected dates of all the periods when she is due to come into season and work out exactly when it is convenient for you to have a litter of puppies. There is no point, for example, in mating your dog and then realizing that there is a family holiday booked a week after the puppies are born.

A few weeks before she is expected to come on heat, make an appointment with your vet and ask him to check her over. If the bitch has any traces of worms or irritations which will require treatment, now is the time to carry them out, not when she is expecting, because to give drugs then may cause deformities in the unborn puppies. Overweight bitches stand a good chance of being temporarily infertile and the veterinary surgeon will be able to advise on the ideal weight for your dog.

The season lasts for 21 days with the maximum period of fertility occurring between day nine and day 14. Although it is possible for a successful mating to be carried out at

any time during this fertile period, day 11 is usually considered to be the optimum. There are, of course, exceptions to every rule.

The physical signs of when a bitch is coming on heat are a slight swelling of the vulva from which appears a light bloody discharge. This will eventually become clear fluid and, by the 11th day, if you stroke or scratch the bitch around the base of her tail, you will notice that she stands with her tail well over to one side. She is, at this stage, very definitely, ready for

By scratching the bitch at the base of her tail, you can tell if she is ready for mating.

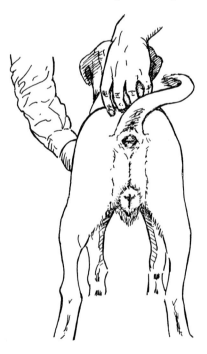

mating.

If it is possible to allow both bitch and potential stud dog out together for a period of time over several days, the bitch will soon let the handler know when she is ready.

The actual mating procedure is not necessarily an easy operation, especially if one or both of the dogs are inexperienced. The best way to effect a mating, at least as an initial approach, is to put both dog and bitch in a large kennel or loose box. Let them run about and get to know each other but keep your eye on them without interfering. If the bitch stands but then gets frustrated due to the inexpertise of the stud dog, or the dog himself shows very little interest, do not leave them too long before parting them and trying them again the following day.

It is not, as so many people seem to think, necessary for a 'tie' to take place for the mating to be successful but this is usually the eventual outcome. This tie can last a considerable length of time and the dog will effect this by mounting the bitch in the conventional way before turning himself round to face the opposite direction to the bitch. During this period, the sperm is flowing from the dog to the bitch and obviously indicates the likelihood of a more successful mating than one which is over in a matter of seconds or minutes.

TRAINERS' TIPS

- Most bitches will mate successfully on the 11th, 12th and 13th day. A smear test carried out by your vet will tell you when the bitch is ovulating and the correct time for mating.

- Be sure of your dates – it is a pretty safe bet that the bitch has been on heat at least a couple of days longer than one thinks. Also, prepare the potential stud dog well in advance.

- Some bitches will mate as early as the fifth day and as late as the 18th day. Some bitches may also have to be held as they will never mate freely.

- There is a school of thought which believes that after mating, the bitch should not be worked or given any strenuous exercise for a few days as there is a faint danger of her returning sperm. But surely, once the egg has been fertilized there can be no turning back?

MISSING GAME

If your dog misses game when competing at a field trial, he would be eliminated or at least marked down. How can I ensure that this never happens to me and my spaniel?

You cannot ensure that this this will never happen. Even a normally good game finder will sometimes miss game due to poor scenting conditions. Poor scent can be caused by a multitude of reasons, ranging from the weather, through to livestock fouling any ground scent. Bracken, dead leaves, and a field of kale or some other strongly scented crop are some more, if less obvious ones, whilst artificial fertilizers, chemicals and recent dung-spreading activities have also been found to be detrimental to scent.

Gundog handlers with experience of the grouse moors will already know just how poor scenting can be when the ground is very dry and there is a lot of warm sunshine, especially when the heather is in full bloom and the pollen kills any chance the dog may have of picking up any scent at all.

It is also evident, from experience in the fox-hunting field and taking note of the experiences of various huntsmen, that what starts out as a screaming scent on grassland will often change as the quarry takes hounds across a ploughed field or into marshy ground. The explanation put forward in such circumstances is that the grassland could be warmer than the air at the same time that the other type of ground is cooler. Conversely, it could be expected that scenting will be poor when these conditions are reversed and the air is warmer than the ground.

Returning to the world of gundogs, however, one occasionally finds that game can be missed through the dog working the ground at too great a speed. You must therefore try to slow

TRAINERS' TIPS

- You should be in a position to trust your dog after attaining field-trial level but if there is any suspicion of impending poor scent (which may be observed when out on early morning exercise), make every effort to slow the dog down.

- The only thing that can be done is to ensure that the dog works a good tight pattern and is encouraged to investigate every bit of cover that may hold game. Also (at field trials) the rate the line is moving must be regulated to allow dogs time to do this.

down the dog and this can best be done by encouraging the animal to maintain a tight pattern whilst quartering. Some days it will be noticed that game is sitting very tightly – very often this too is a result of weather conditions. If this is suspected to be the case, do not allow the dog to range too far as game may well be right under your feet.

MOUTHING

From talking to fellow golden retriever owners in my local gundog club, it appears that I am not alone in experiencing this apparently 'good' fault. What can I do when I notice my bitch continually put down a retrieve in order to get a better grip?

Before going more deeply into the subject, it is as well to get the mouth question into perspective. To this end I quote a passage written in 1929 by Vincent Routledge:

> As although nobody appreciates a soft and velvety mouth more than the writer, still the primary use of a retriever is to bring game to hand, and it is surely better to recover it, even if it should be mauled a little, than to leave wounded birds out to die a lingering death.

Although writing of hard mouth, Mr Routledge's comments apply equally as well to mouthing. It is obviously a problem for a young dog to work well towards a pricked-bird and subsequently make a retrieve, only to drop it and let a lightly wounded bird run several yards in search of dense and protective cover.

Professional trainers do not

Most young dogs handle their first few retrieves with undue sensitivity.

consider this to be too much of a problem and believe that most young dogs have this favourable peculiarity. Experience states that these habits disappear after a few days picking-up and, provided that the dog is at the required level of training, after he has retrieved a few runners.

TRAINERS' TIPS

- It is also a good idea to blow the re-call whistle and then turn and walk away as soon as the dog picks the bird. This will encourage a fast return which is obviously desirable.

- On the rare occasions when a dog persists with this problem, it will pay to practise a few retrieves from cover over longer distances.

NERVOUSNESS

Out on her own, my young pointer bitch works very well. In company, however (when I want to show off her progress to my friends and family), she tends to hang back and is not quite as bold. Obviously, she will eventually be working in company and I wonder how best to cure this general nervousness.

General nervousness, as opposed to *gun-nervousness* (see p.43) should not occur with a puppy which has been bred from working parents and, in the opinion of the professionals, is usually a result of bad breeding.

Nervousness should not, however, be confused with sensitivity which is a totally different matter. The dog in this particular query seems to fall into the latter category and, as groups of people seem to confuse this bitch, it would make sense for the owner to spend some time in taking the dog to events and shopping areas where large numbers of people are present.

Likewise, although it might be supposed that a working gundog never needs to come into contact with heavy traffic, there will eventually come a time when a bird needs to be picked or flushed alongside the road.

The dangers of such an operation are obvious but in practice, if a dog is to be of any use workwise, he must be familiar with traffic. A dog of a nervy or sensitive disposition sent to retrieve and then frightened by a passing

TRAINERS' TIPS

- This can be helped by humanization. From eight weeks of age try to have the dog around with you as much as possible.

- Expose the dog to different situations. Introduce them to people, riding in the car, and have him in the house so that he gets used to sudden sounds.

vehicle may well be distracted to the extent that he runs towards the danger rather than away. Time spent in ensuring that the dog is fully confident in and around traffic will pay dividends.

Very young dogs can be made nervous by stupidity. Instances where shotguns have been fired over eight-week-old puppies in order to test them for gun-shyness have been recorded!

OBESITY

Despite being well exercised, my dog is getting fat. What could be the reason and how can I rectify the problem?

If a dog is fat, it is usually due to diet and the type of food available, although it could also be caused by spaying or castration. Regular exercise will help but all the exercise in the world will not run the fat off a dog unless there is a balanced diet being fed at the same time.

Some of the all-in-one foods previously recommended (see *feeding*, p.38) do, unfortunately, contain a high calorie content and if this is suspected to be the case, it will obviously pay to change to a lower carbohydrate food. Never do this overnight, however, as a sudden

A dog which is overweight, and uncomfortable as a result, cannot be expected to work well. Obesity could, therefore, be a cause of unexpected problems.

TRAINERS' TIPS

- Try one of the special diets available from the vet.

- Give plenty of exercise, and cut down on food.

- Cut down or change the food until the required balance is achieved.

- You might think the dog is well exercised but is that by your standards rather than his? It is reckoned that sheepdogs working on the moors run 14 miles to each one which the shepherd walks. Does your exercise routine match this or is your dog ambling along at your heel?

change in diet could lead to yet more problems.

Very occasionally, obesity cannot be corrected no matter how careful you are with both diet and exercise, because of the dog's metabolism.

Regular exercise will help in preventing obesity. Naturally 'lazy' dogs may, however, need to be encouraged into free-running exercise so they are not continually around your heels.

VETERINARY COMMENT

Obesity is defined as the condition in which the body weight of a dog is 10 per cent or more over what is normal for a particular breed. In general terms, however, if you cannot feel a dog's ribs, it is obese.

Obese dogs have shorter lives because they suffer from sugar diabetes, arthritis, heart and respiratory disorders. Occasionally they prove to be more irritable and this is obviously not a good thing when dealing with generally mild-mannered gundog breeds.

Obesity tends to arise with the advent of middle age. (I find it interesting to note that many obese and middle-aged owners arrive at my surgery with obese and middle-aged dogs!)

Establish a target weight, perhaps from books dealing with breed standards. The dog should then be fed an amount of food which will provide 60 per cent of the energy requirement of a normal dog.

I personally would recommend 'crash dieting' but find that most owners think this cruel and will not stick to the diet I suggest.

OVER-BREAKING

Someone has lent me an old book on spaniel training. In it the author refers to 'over-breaking' but does not explain what he means. I presume this is a fault.

H W Carlton in his 1915 classic *Spaniels, Their Breaking for Sport and Field Trials* explains the term:

> . . . instil into the puppy's mind that you are not a hard task master, but are the benefactor on whose will its pleasure depends, and that it is to you that it must look, both mentally and physically for such pleasure as it may enjoy. When therefore, you keep it waiting on its bench for dinner . . . wait until it has turned its eyes to you before you gratify its desires. When you come to hunting this paves the way for that watching you with half an eye that prevents its getting out of range . . . This does not mean that the dog is to stop and look at you for orders, a fault often seen at field trials, and probably due to over-breaking.

Over-breaking is, therefore, merely another term for a dog which because of boredom has become dull and over-reliant on his handler.

P

PEGGING GAME

Although I am not too worried about the fact, my springer when out beating sometimes manages to catch or 'peg' more pheasants than the guns shoot! I have no intention of doing any field trialing with this dog.

Some dogs become remarkably adept at pegging game. Usually it is pheasants which have squatted under cover rather than running forward to the flushing points which get caught but occasionally rabbits too will be collected by an over-zealous dog.

What to do with a bird that has been pegged is another matter but I personally always kill a pheasant picked by my spaniels and always ask my beaters to do the same. This is not in order to bump up the bag, but because although outwardly there might appear to be no damage to the bird, even the softest-mouthed spaniel may damage the internal organs in the effort of picking up or retrieving from cover. Also, although it may be obvious that the bird has not been shot at during this drive, it could have been shot and wounded on a previous occasion and may perhaps still be

TRAINERS' TIPS

- This is a grey area. When I judge a field trial I now give the benefit of the doubt and ask the handler of a dog which I suspect to have pegged a bird to send his dog out again. If, however, there is a possible fault, I can only suggest that the handler attempts to reach his dog before he pegs a bird and then flushes it himself.

  He would need to be aware of the workings of the dog in order to do so but, in any event, it will help towards steadiness if nothing else. The ideal would be to let the bird fly off unharmed.

carrying a blood scent.

Interestingly enough, it seems to be spaniels, rather than any other breeds, which fall foul of this problem. Hen pheasants rather than cocks seem more likely to be pegged.

Field trial judges vary in their opinion of how best to treat a dog which has pegged a bird. At one time such a misdemeanour would have meant automatic elimination but it appears that these rulings have been changed, giving the benefit of the doubt to the dog who, after all, is more able than them to scent a bird which has been pricked.

PICKING-UP

I have been asked picking-up by the keeper in charge of the neighbouring shoot. Although flattered at being asked to take a 'step up the ladder', I must admit to being a little worried as to my responsibilities.

Picking-up is, to my mind, the most important factor in running a shoot. The keeper may have a plentiful supply of birds and the guns may be excellent shots but if there is no-one there who can pick-up cleanly, humanely and efficiently, both are likely to be disappointed.

A keeper needs to show birds and have plenty of game in the bag at the end of the day. The guns need to show off their prowess and the only way they can do this is to be able to say and see that there is the expected amount of game in the larder at the end of the day.

In this present economic climate, most shoots need to let a few days in order to cover the cost of the guest or regular syndicate members which have, until recently, been the norm. Co-operative or roving syndicates appear on the shoot and neither the host nor his keeper and beaters know

the standard of marksmanship likely to appear. Pickers-up can help but only if the guns understand why they are there.

A team of pickers-up must have a leader. He must be at the appointed meeting-place in plenty of time and have been made aware of the intended drives in order that the keeper can concentrate on beaters and 'stops'.

The host, who is naturally fraught and wishes to give his guests a good day, is concentrating on a smoothly run operation. He is not, therefore, likely to be pleased by pickers-up who do not know what they are doing and show themselves frequently.

The distance that a picker-up should position himself from the guns depends greatly on the type of shooting undertaken. On the grouse or partridge shoot, a picker-up would need to stand much further back than he would on a pheasant shoot where, because of the close proximity of cover, there is always the danger of interfering with a future drive.

A potentially dangerous gun may turn around and see a picker-up in his sights. With luck he will have the sense to withdraw his gun; if he is not automatically aware of the potential danger, he should not have been included in the first place.

TRAINERS' TIPS

- Take note of the local grapevine. If the shoot involved has a bad name, don't be tempted into picking-up there.

- Try and speak to the leader of the picking-up team beforehand. He will tell you what is expected of you.

- Many shoots have difficulty in finding pickers-up and have to advertise in magazines such as *The Shooting Times*. A good shoot would have a waiting-list of beaters and pickers-up. It does, however depend on the area in which you live and operate. The affluent south is more likely to have waiting-lists than the more remote and less commercially viable areas of Britain.

POINTING

My spaniel points naturally which I find very useful on our rough shoot but a little annoying when beating on a large local estate as we always seem to get left behind by the line! Should I encourage or discourage this habit?

The question of pointing is entirely a matter of personal preference. On a rough shoot where the opportunity for a shot may be limited it is obviously advantageous to own a dog which will, upon scenting game, point long enough for the gun to get into the best possible position. Although spaniels and retrieving breeds will sometimes do this naturally, it is unlikely that they will 'hold a point' for very long. Sometimes, however, this period of time can be extended when through experience, the dog learns to wait for a further command from the handler before rushing in to the flush.

Pointers and setters will, through careful and selective breeding, advance slowly upon the winded quarry and stand indefinitely. But to expect any of the other breeds to do the same generally wastes time and is also apt to develop into pointing at places where fur or feather has recently been, rather than where they are at the present moment – in other words, false pointing.

On the plus side, a rough shooter's dog which does point, is unlikely to spoil a potential shot nor get too far ahead of the beating line. It is therefore, perhaps a shame that this particular quality cannot be tested at

TRAINERS' TIPS

● It is no good expecting a spaniel or retriever to do the work normally performed by a pointer. The latter's sole job is to find game and indicate its whereabouts by either 'coming up on point', or 'setting'.

● If it is considered desirable, pointing in spaniels can be encouraged during training, especially if a rabbit pen is available. If the puppy under tuition becomes rigid in a pointing attitude when he/she finds a rabbit, I go up as quickly and quietly as I can and take hold of the check cord, drawing it tight and keeping the dog in position for as long as possible. Eventually, the pupil will make

a dive for the rabbit and I then give the command to drop. In order to retain this pointing tendency, it is necessary to prevent their flushing the quarry every time.

● This query is somewhat akin to the one dealt with in the section on dropping to command and/or shot. On a rough shoot it is possible whereas on a shoot where large numbers are seen, the handler of a spaniel which points would still be working his/her way through the first drive when the other guns and beaters were going in for lunch! (See also *dropping to command/shot*, p.34, *standing*, p.104, *quartering*, p.83).

a field trial. (This does not, of course apply to trials runs for pointers and setters where their ability to come on point is marked very highly.)

In America, trial rules for spaniels insist that the approach to game must be both firm and definite. Any hesitation on the approach is severely penalized. In this country the situation is somewhat different and, as a general rule, no judge would mark down a dog until the point is held so long that it serves no useful pupose.

POISONS

A friend of mine's terrier has just died from eating rat poison. This has naturally upset my wife who is now worried that every time I take our labrador out on a shooting day, he will pick up something which may prove fatal. What potential dangers should I look out for?

It should not be necessary to point out that all obvious poisons around the kennels must be kept under lock and key but there are many less obvious sources which may prove fatal.

A selection of potential poisons together with, on the left, possible antidotes, including milk, vinegar and baking powder.

VETERINARY COMMENTS

Some of the most common forms of non-caustic poisons are strychnine put out for moles, agricultural chemicals, dressed seed and antifreeze. It might be argued that no dog in his right senses would willingly lap up the latter but it is not generally known that antifreeze is in fact a very sweet-tasting substance and, judging by the entries in many veterinary day-books, is a regular source of poisoning. Washing soda given to the patient will help before veterinary advice is sought.

Caustic poisoning is a different proposition and washing soda given to induce vomiting will only worsen the situation due to the passage of the poison back through the trachea and soft palate. Instead, the poison should be diluted whilst in the stomach by giving milk in the case of an acidic poison or, for those of an alkaline nature, a solution of vinegar or lemon juice. Likely caustic poisons are kerosene, battery acid, barbiturates and acetic acids.

In all cases, the idea is to prevent absorption into the bloodstream but the above should only be used as intermediate measures before seeking professional help.

POTTERING

My dog tends to potter when I take him out shooting, much to my and my shooting companions' annoyance. Is there anything I can do?

Not dissimilar to *laziness* (see p.59), the fault of pottering causes annoyance to the handler and all those watching. Like laziness, it is usually found in show-bred dogs where most of the working instinct has been bred out of them.

A good working type will almost always want to please (although dogs can have 'off-days' as well as handlers!) and thoroughly enjoys its training and subsequent work with the gun.

Pottering can also be caused by a boring training routine and if a dog was initially keen and stylish, it should, with a little time and effort, be possible to rectify the problem.

A born 'potterer' on the other hand is a frustrating piece of work, ambling from side to side and showing no real enthusiasm. In the opinion of at least one professional, the owner of such an animal would do almost as well by leaving the dog at home and kicking through the cover himself. And H W Carlton certainly agreed on this point:

> To the man who goes out 'spanieling' for his own amusement, I fancy that pottering annoys him more than passing stuff – the pottering is a visible source of annoyance all the time, whereas the stuff his dog has missed might, for all he knows, not be there at all. Personally . . . I would rather shoot over a dog that goes a good pace.

TRAINERS' TIPS

- A dog which has only recently developed this problem should be taken onto gamey ground and the training routine made more interesting.

- If the dog is dwelling on a scent or place which clearly cannot hold any game, call him off immediately.

- The safest rule is, I think, to err rather on the side of calling your dog off too soon than on that of letting him dwell upon the scent too long.

- Pottering in a gundog is an abomination to be avoided at all costs.

PSYCHOLOGY

What exactly is meant by psychology in connection with gundog training?

The Pocket Oxford Dictionary defines psychology as being 'science of . . . mind. Investigating interaction of conscious and unconscious element in the mind'.

As with any breed of dog it is vital that the gundog owner tries to understand exactly what is going on in the animal's head. It is all too easy to anthropomorphize and, because of their apparent ability to understand, credit gundogs with being responsible for their actions. In actual fact, nothing could be further from the truth even though the aim of training is to control bodily actions through the medium of the dog's mind.

One of the first requirements is to become the centre of interest to the dog and this is why so many professional gundog trainers insist on their animals being kennelled when not out exercising or training. A lack of attention may arise from many circumstances, some of which can be attributed to fear of the owner, being too immature, boredom or even ill health.

Because of a lack of reasoning power, instinct has to be modified by experience rather than by reason. At all times, it is easier to obtain the desired response immediately rather than to allow faults to develop and then try to eradicate them before

endeavouring to form new ones.

It is convenient that this section immediately precedes the one dealing with punishment as no better example of psychological understanding can be given. The act of punishing a dog not only shows that 'master' is displeased but also establishes the dog owner as pack leader.

If you watch dogs, wolves or large cats 'playing', it will not be long before one will be seen attacking the other's throat or neck area. By chastising a dog in the way described by the professional trainers – picking

When it is necessary to punish a dog, a good shaking is far more effective than a beating. Make sure the dog is caught in the act before chastizing. He will then realize what he is being punished for.

TRAINERS' TIPS

- Where possible, the young gundog should be allowed to try and solve his own problems as this is the quickest way of learning and allowing the dog to develop his instinct and intelligence.

- Dogs cannot be trained by means of a crash course and if you have any hopes at all of achieving a useful, working ally, an inexhaustible amount of patience is essential.

- Failures and disappointments should be avoided but are impossible without the owner having at least some understanding of how the gundog's mind works.

up and shaking – the same impression is being given. In breeds which are too heavy to pick up, the same effect can be achieved by grabbing hold of the loose skin at either side of the neck and staring into the eyes.

PUNISHMENT

Expecting the worst, I know that when I eventually begin training my labrador puppy, there will be times when she does wrong and I will have to punish her. How is this best administered and how do I avoid breaking the bond that she and I have already created?

The old breed of Victorian dog breakers believed that the dogs in their charge should be allowed to run wild and chase as much as opportunity allowed up until the age of 12 months. They would then begin training by means of a stick and attempt to knock out the faults whilst hoping to leave the good points. If the hitherto, riotous, puppy was at all nervous, the sudden check which he received upon reaching the magic 12 months was often enough to break his spirit.

Thankfully, today's trainers and the methods developed by their predecessors over the last 60 or 70 years, are considerably less barbaric and involve understanding the dog's mind as well as being sure that the dog understands the commands given by the handler.

There is, however, one subject where some of today's would-be trainers fall into the same trap of ignorance as did the Victorian 'bully' and this is in the area of administering punishment.

It is not uncommon to see intelligent and normally logical owners beat the hell out of their dog when he returns from running-in rather than run out and catch the dog

TRAINERS' TIPS

- Beating should never be necessary. If you are strong enough pick the dog up and shake him.

- Pick the dog up by the loose skin of the throat and give him a good shake and chastise the dog by growling in a gruff voice.

- If a dog disobeys the 'stop' whistle, run out to the dog and catch him. Take him to the spot where the misdeed occurred and shake him by the scruff of the neck at the same time looking into his eyes.

in the act. If the dog in question has run-in to retrieve and is then chastised upon his return, he is, in his mind, being punished for his last act and that was, of course, retrieving. No wonder then, when he is next sent out he shows a reluctance to return.

In nine cases out of ten, wrongly administered punishment can be put down to a loss of temper on the part of the owner, but once a lack of understanding occurs there is little time for remorse and it will be necessary to work hard on rebuilding the bond between dog and trainer.

All agree that, should punishment be necessary, it must be administered both *in the act of doing wrong* and *on the spot where it occurred*.

QUARTERING

My spaniel works well enough when rough-shooting on my own but when beating on the local shoot he tends to run ahead. Why? How can I correct this?

Ideally, to be a really effective aid to sport, the spaniel should work a strip – with the trainer walking up the centre – 30 or 40 yards wide, first hunting all likely cover on one side, then crossing in front of the handler to work on the other. He should then continue to cross back and forth until the particular drive is finished. The speed at which the dog moves will, of course, depend on scenting ability but he should be as speedy and stylish as possible without running the risk of *missing game* (see p.66).

Training manuals suggest that you should walk into the wind and quarter it yourself in short beats. By holding your hand out, preferably not very far from the ground, get the dog out beyond you in the direction across the wind that you are going. As soon as he has got out, call the dog's name and turn sharply in the contrary direction across the wind, repeating

these movements until the end of the beat.

So far so good, but whilst both in training and on the rough-shoot, the handler is walking at the dog's pace. It is a different matter when beating in line. Most beating lines walk too quickly, not giving the dog the chance to work. I do not know a keeper or his employer who would allow it but, to prevent a spaniel from running ahead, the only real answer is to slow the line down and insist on the dog stopping to flush. If this were carried out in practice, however, a shoot where birds were plentiful would still only be half-way through the first drive by lunch-time!

You should also be wary of taking a well-trained spaniel onto a shoot where all the other dogs in the line are wild. It is an unfortunate fact that even the best-trained spaniel will revert when there is a competitive

element attached.

A young dog may go one of two ways on his first foray onto the shooting field. If he is of a sensitive disposition he may well hold back, in which case it is a simple matter of gentle encouragement; or he may, because of the excitement of seeing other dogs working, the noise of beaters and the sound of gunfire, forget his quartering lessons and run ahead as described by the questioner.

When working in a beating line, there is a tendency for a questing dog to forget his early lessons and run ahead in order to keep up with the line: the more he develops the fault of working in front, the more acute the angle of quartering should be made.

TRAINERS' TIPS

- Where possible, work the dog on the hedgerow or edge of the wood to one side of the beating line so that you can concentrate on him.

- Go back to basic quartering lessons – the greater tendency your dog displays to work on in front of you instead of quartering his ground, the more acute you should make the angle of your own quarterings so that you are almost walking back onto the line of the previous beat.

- As your dog gradually gets to understand what is required of him, make your own quarterings shorter and shorter until you are walking in a straight line.

QUIVERING

Though outwardly healthy, I am a little worried by the fact that my cocker spaniel bitch looks so unhappy and cold when I pick-up at our neighbouring shoot. Is she unwell or, being a very small cocker, simply exhausted?

It is unlikely that a well-trained and correctly exercised dog of the right working strain will be either unsettled or unhappy on the shooting day.

When a regular member of a picking-up team, especially if it is a large shoot, there is a temptation to send the dog off for more retrieves than he can comfortably manage. Common sense must come into play and, even though you might feel that you are not 'pulling your weight', rest assured that once the problem is explained, other members of the team will help out. Several dogs in the kennel give the handler more choice in selecting a particular retrieve for a particular animal and when one tires, another can take his place.

Spaniels, no matter which type, have the unfortunate habit of looking appealing and 'hard-done-by' but sympathy in their case is wasted and you are worrying unnecessarily if they 'quiver' only on a shooting day.

TRAINERS' TIPS

- I am willing to bet that it is nothing more than tension and excitement which causes 'quivering'.

RABBIT PENS

I am considering building a rabbit pen. Are they any use in avoiding potential problems in training and have you any comments regarding their construction?

Most professional gundog trainers feel the need to construct and use a pen on their premises. If spoken to nicely they will usually allow a novice dog and handler to use it under supervision. For the one-dog trainer, this solution may be far simpler than going to the trouble and expense of contructing your own.

It is generally thought a rabbit pen can be most beneficial in the training of a gundog. However, they should be used sparingly so as not to let the dog in question become too familiar with either the pen itself or its occupants. As with the over-frequent use of a check-cord, a dog will very quickly become aware of its limitations and will soon learn that it cannot get away with chasing within the restricted area that a rabbit pen affords. Back out in the wide open spaces, however, it is not unusual to find the trainee reverting to his bad

habits.

As to construction, a pen should be as large as possible in area. The materials used are generally wooden fencing stakes which, in order to prevent the fence collapsing once the straining and enclosing wire is attached, need to be strutted. When building an ordinary fence, corner struts would normally be made from wooden stakes nailed and angled at around 30 degrees. With a rabbit pen, these corner struts need some careful consideration as, if set at the wrong angle or too far away from the fencing line, they offer an excellent means of escape. In order to overcome this, supporting struts made from twisted straining wire would probably be better.

Straining wire along the top and bottom will help in achieving the correct degree of tautness and this is quite important as rabbits are capable of scrambling up wire which is too slack. The enclosing fence itself is normally made up of one-inch chicken wire around four feet in height and with a turn-over at the top of one foot. This 'flap' will deflect the rabbits should they attempt to jump out.

At the base of the fence, another flap of one foot should be turned inwards so as to prevent the inmates from being able to dig out. Any straining wire left over should be cut into short lengths and bent into an inverted 'U' shape. These will serve as cheap and efficient pegs. At the risk of insulting the reader's intelligence it may nevertheless be as well to point out that a six-foot roll of netting will

be required to build a fence line of the height described.

Beware of any old stumps within close reach of the fence line as rabbits will also use these as jumping-out platforms.

Once constructed, it will obviously be necessary to beg, borrow or steal a selection of rabbits with which to begin one's colony. Wild rabbits would perhaps be best as they are the type the dog is likely to encounter naturally. Domesticated stock are, however, almost as good, but try and

When erecting a rabbit pen, be sure either to dig in the wire at the base or fold it inwards to prevent escapees. Incorrectly angled corner struts will provide a ramp from which rabbits can leap.

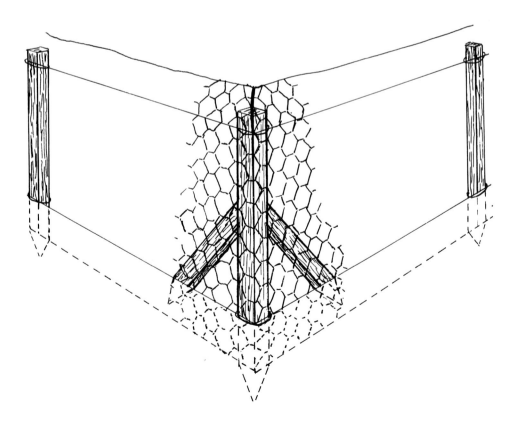

avoid most coloured ones and, if there is a choice, choose those nearest in colour to the wild rabbits as possible. Tame rabbits also have the advantage of settling into their new surroundings better than any wild ones which you may be fortunate enough to obtain. They should be fed in the same way as you would feed a pet animal but if the pen is large enough and contains a fair amount of natural vegetation, they may not need feeding in all but the hardest winter weather.

If you have not enclosed any existing cover – brambles, tussacky grass and the like – place plenty of fir boughs, straw bales and other cover in the pen so that the rabbits can have some protection in bad weather and also get away from the dogs.

Where foxes are a problem, it may pay to include a low electric fence around the outside of the perimeter as a fox could jump in and out of a four-foot high fence with very little trouble.

TRAINERS' TIPS

- Ten minutes per session is plenty.

- Spaniels require quite a large pen; retrievers can get away with a smaller one.

- If a dog is known to be very keen, place a check-cord or long lead around its neck for the first few sessions.

- When the pupil is a little too keen and attempts either to chase or move from the 'hup' position as rabbits are perhaps being walked past him, blow the 'stop' whistle and make sure he obeys immediately.

- If a rabbit pen cannot be found in your area, look for a keeper with a pen of laying pheasants. When laying has finished and there is no risk of disturbing the birds, he may be prepared to let you take the dog into the pen and walk the pheasants around. Whilst obviously not as good as a rabbit pen, it goes a long way towards making a dog steady to game.

RAW MEAT

Every year I walk a couple of foxhound puppies for the local hunt. They supply me with as much raw meat as I need to feed them. As the price of all-in-one dog feeds have risen recently, I was contemplating using some of the surplus meat to offset the cost of feeding my two gundogs. Is this a good idea?

Unpleasant though the feeding of flesh and offal may at first seem, it pays to remember that dogs are, relatively speaking, still very close to nature in their pack and feeding habits. Huskies are a good example and although domesticated still retain a fair proportion of their natural metabolism – so much so that many interested modern-day breeders have found it beneficial to feed their dogs raw rabbit still 'in the skin' so that they can obtain the necessary roughage.

You should not, however, take the above as meaning that raw rabbit meat, chicken or other meat can be fed to any of the gundog breeds as there is always the obvious danger of small bones splintering and becoming stuck in the dog's throat, causing death by choking.

Green tripe and paunch is rather revolting from the human point of view but, to dogs, it makes the ideal meal and is readily taken on board. In the wild, lions will rip out and eat the stomachs of their quarry before moving on to the red meat. Both tripe and paunch are full of low protein and can be given throughout a dog's life. Because of the protein factor, however, it should ideally be mixed with cereals such as flaked maize, rolled oats and rolled wheat. Even then, the mix is still not quite sufficient for a working dog and will require the addition of sterilized bonemeal (not the kind used by gardeners!). Ox tripe contains more suet and so will not require the addition of as much cereal.

If you decide to feed your dog on meat and offal, it should be remembered that though generally more beneficial than tins of processed meat and expensive biscuit, this kind of diet is likely to cause more problems with worms than you would normally expect.

It has to be said that, in this day and age, it is usually only hunting establishments, for the most part, that give their hounds a break from red meat at least once a week, substituting either a cereal porridge or paunches from casualties collected that week from the local farmers. Others starve their hounds for one day a week, feeling that it gives the digestive system an all-important rest. This is, once again, not too far removed from the way in which dogs would have behaved in the wild as it is unlikely that they would have been successful in killing every day.

The way in which raw meat is given varies from hunt to hunt, some merely skinning a carcass and letting the hounds rip the meat from the bones, others cutting off slices of meat and using the bones as stock for the cereal porridge. One professional gundog trainer to whom I talked and who insists on the old-fashioned methods of feeding, believes that the latter system should be taken a stage further and the strips of meat be minced as, because of the pack instinct, the dog has to eat quickly. Having been minced, the food can then be gulped down at a rapid rate. Whether this is really necessary to the owner with only a couple of gundogs is open to doubt, but it is nevertheless an interesting school of thought.

If you only own a couple of gundogs, the trouble involved in getting hold of farm casualties, skinning and jointing them for the freezer and then finding a way of getting rid of the skin and bones, is not likely to be worthwhile. If associated to a local hunt, however, the feeding of raw meat may be a reasonable proposition.

TRAINERS' TIPS

- Green tripe is readily available from most pet suppliers and comes quite cheaply in pre-packed blocks which can be kept in the household freezer. It does, however, have one minor disadvantage. Once it has defrosted it smells revolting and what is more, the dog will soon begin to smell the same way. This may not be too much of a problem with a dog which is kennelled outside but is not too pleasant a prospect when keeping a house dog.

- Red meat is a useful and healthy food but, in the opinion of most vets and experienced dog owners, should not be given without a break as it is thought to have a toxic effect upon the dog's kidney.

RETRIEVING

I take my black labrador bitch to the Welney Marshes. Although generally good at retrieving, she will sometimes let me down by refusing to pick-up over water. To make matters worse, she has the embarrassing habit of preferring to pick-up plastic milk bottles (of which, for some reason, there appear to be a great many), causing as might be imagined, much amusement amongst my shooting colleagues!

Many of the faults associated with retrieving have been dealt with in the section headed *delivery* (see p.29) but there are at least three further potential difficulties which are best itemized as specific retrieving problems. The first of these concerns dogs which although keen initially to go out and retrieve, then spit out the dummy or bird.

Almost all dogs will, when retrieving from water, pause upon reaching dry land and shake themselves. Sometimes they drop whatever they are carrying before picking it up and carrying it back to the handler without further mishap. If the bird is a runner there is obviously a problem when a dog persists in this annoying habit but, nine times out of ten, he will soon learn to hold onto a bird which is obviously wounded although he may continue putting down a dead bird before ridding himself of excess water.

Actually spitting out a bird and refusing to pick it up again is, however, a totally different matter and could be caused by over-retrieving early on in training. By throwing objects repeatedly, the dog begins to spit them out in readiness for another retrieve.

Secondly, a dog which retrieves the dummy and then proceeds to stand there shaking it may be doing this for a number of reasons. First, in the wild this is a method of killing quarry by breaking the neck; secondly, retrieving training might have been treated too much like a game; and thirdly, he might have been made over-excited by being engaged in a tug-of-war when the retrieve was being taken away from him. (Never, attempt to snatch or grab a dummy from a dog. If he seems reluctant to hand over, place the finger and thumb of one hand under the jaw and *gently* prise the jaws apart. Some trainers suggest pressing the dog's lips against its teeth by the same action.)

Finally, some young dogs will get bored with dummy work and refuse to retrieve. The obvious answer when this is suspected is to change from dummies to the real thing. Initially, they should not be allowed to pick-up freshly shot and therefore, warm game. An occasional retrieve with a cleanly shot, cold and undamaged bird will often regenerate the

TRAINERS' TIPS

- The problem of spitting out the dummy is quite a common one in retrieves from water. If this is the case, as the dog comes out of the water with the dummy in his mouth, the trainer should call him by name and then turn and run away. As the dog comes up to you (as he surely will), turn quickly and take the dummy.

- If this problem persists then the dog must be taught the command 'hold' by placing the dummy in the dog's mouth and making him hold the dummy until required. This will also work with a dog that shakes the dummy.

- With a dog which doesn't like feathers, use cold game and place a rubber band around the wings. Tuck the bird's head into the rubber band. Alternatively, tie a set of pheasant wings around a dummy which you know from past experience, the dog likes retrieving. Never use a pigeon (unless enclosed within a sock or foot piece cut from a stocking or pair of tights), as their feathers are very loose and a mouth full of feathers can upset the dog, who will spit out the bird in an effort to rid himself of feathers.

retrieving interest and once this is found to be the case, retrieving practice should be given very sparingly in future. Conversely, a dog may be happy enough to retrieve a dummy but is reluctant to pick up anything which has feathers.

Once a dog is proficient at retrieving, only give the occasional retrieve in subsequent lessons. To do so will only create further problems such as playing with the dummy and/or reluctance to return to the handler.

REWARDS

In an effort to encourage my dog to retrieve the dummy quickly and efficiently, I have got into the habit of offering her a tit-bit. Unfortunately she now drops the dummy in anticipation of her reward.

A dog which is bred from good working stock and has, during its first few weeks in a new home, been 'humanized', should form a bond between himself and his trainer. Once formal training begins the dog should then be only too eager to please his handler and should not need the enticement of tit-bits.

The only exceptions to this rule could be during these self-same early stages when tit-bits may possibly encourage a sensitive puppy to come back to the handler. As soon as this has been accomplished however, it should be sufficient to reward by words and hand contact.

While on the subject of a verbal 'reward', never be frightened of appearing stupid or silly to onlookers: it is far more important to establish a rapport with the puppy than to worry about what people think. The best way to let a dog know that you are pleased with him or her is first of all to bend down so that you do not seem so tall and formidable and then to speak to them encouragingly and in a higher pitch than you would normally speak. It matters not what you say so long as it is obvious that you are happy. Once again, take a leaf from the hunting world and the professional huntsman who is continually encouraging his hounds to try their best even on a bad scenting day, caring little what people think.

As to bodily contact, on a hot summer's day, rolling about on the lawn with a new puppy can do wonders in creating a bond between dog and trainer. The late Barbara Woodhouse, an acknowledged expert in general dog training for many years, used to advise her clients, both personally and in her television appearances, to tickle the dog's chest. I personally have found that fondling the ears of any animal, be it dog, cat or horse, gives a favourable response.

The main thing is to be naturally relaxed and approachable. It is no good pretending to be at ease when in reality, you are tense or nervous. Any sensible dog will be aware of these reactions and act accordingly.

Pieces of biscuit and the like (H W Carlton suggests fried liver or even cheese) can, however, be used to get a spaniel hunting. By throwing the biscuit into longish grass and encouraging the dog to find it, the puppy will soon learn to watch your hands, an asset which will prove even more useful when the time comes to begin either quartering if dealing with spaniels or long-distance handling and retrieves when training labradors.

TRAINERS' TIPS

- Stop giving the rewards!

- Tit-bits can be very useful in making a puppy come to you readily or to make him watch your hands.

- Concentrate on establishing a good rapport. The dog will then be only too pleased to respond without the need for any edible reward.

- H W Carlton says in *Spaniels, Their Breaking for Sport and Field Trials (1915):*

  Whether it is better to reward the puppy with a piece of biscuit or other dainty, or simply make much of him, is a moot point, in the early days a reward that appeals to his appetite is the more acceptable, and makes the puppy keener to come back to you, on the other hand, if the reward is given every time, the puppy is apt to get into the habit of dropping the object in expectation of the reward, a habit that is most difficult to counteract and will cause you infinite trouble in the future. A middle course is probably the safer; give such a reward the first two or three times, gradually cease doing so, and reserve it for such time – which is almost sure to arrive – as the puppy begins to show a disinclination to return to you.

While useful in initially attracting the attention of a young dog and teaching it the importance of watching the trainer's hands, edible rewards, in the opinion of most professionals, should from then on only be used as a last resort.

RIDING

I am fortunate to own a horse and have plenty of places to ride off-road. In an effort to keep my spaniels fit, I was thinking of taking them with me when out hacking. Could this cause any unforeseen problems?

Even a horse which is known to be 'bomb-proof' can be startled by a sudden, unexpected object in a hedge or along a track. If it happened to be so when the dog is running alongside, it does not require much imagination to think of the likely consequences.

It is, of course, very tempting to exercise both dog and horse together, especially if you have a busy daily schedule. But apart from the obvious potential danger to the spaniel, horse and indeed rider should they all collide, such a practice can cause many problems in training and work.

The rider should be concentrating on the horse he is riding rather than on his dog. The dog will soon realize this and begin ranging further and further, knowing that he is unlikely to be checked. If he is noticed and called back, it is harder to insist that he does so immediately when on horseback than it would be if you were on foot. Likewise should he flush a rabbit or gamebird, it is more difficult to ensure that he does not chase.

The potential dangers of exercising on horseback are all too obvious.

If exercise has to be done other than on foot, take a tip from the hunting fraternity and use a bicycle.

Spaniels, because of their natural instinct to hunt, tend to range out of gunshot distance unless checked. Efficient quartering and questing of the ground can only be achieved by letting the dog work as quickly as its nose will allow (see *quartering*, p.83 and *missing game*, p.66) and much has been made of the need to slow down to the animal's pace. When you are riding, you are, because of the speed of the horse, actually encouraging the dog to run faster, miss game and take a straight line over the beat rather than the desired diagonally zig-zagging lines.

TRAINERS' TIPS

- I would not advise taking any dog, let alone a gundog, out riding. Apart from the danger, it is impossible to insist on heel-work where necessary. What about the risk of causing heart damage and other problems to an unfit dog as he tries to keep up with a strong sixteen-hands horse?

- No! If it is felt necessary to exercise other than on foot, try a bicycle especially now there are mountain bikes available. Road work on quiet country lanes is a good way of hardening pads and strengthening leg muscles but it is best not to have a dog on a lead, in case it cause the rider to lose his balance.

RUNNING-IN

Is it possible to cure a dog which runs-in and if so, what is the remedy?

All gundogs should be steady at all times to both shot and unshot game. Unfortunately, for a variety of reasons, it is a pretty safe bet that all trainers will, at some time or another, experience problems with running-in.

The degree of seriousness of this problem varies. Some dogs will only ever run-in maybe once a day; others only after the bird has been down for some time when patience is running out. Dogs of this temperament cannot, in the opinion of most professions, ever really be trusted not to run-in and certainly will if and when the right occasion arises.

Several years ago, I had an old spaniel who, although steady in the beating line, would insist upon running-in when I was picking-up and a bird was pricked. An unshot bird would be ignored but a wounded one only needed to be carrying a couple of pellets and then crash land into bushes behind the picking-up line and

Where more than one dog is in training or dogs of differing ages are kept, many subjects can be taught. Throwing a dummy over the group can test one for retrieving ability and the others for steadiness.

the spaniel was onto it. His actions pose several questions, not least of which is, 'how did he know a bird was pricked?' It must be virtually impossible to a dog to own a blood scent whilst the bird is still flying but perhaps damaged feathers made the bird sound different from others as it glided through the air. Secondly, should I have tried to correct the fault? To me it didn't matter; it got no worse and was in fact to be encouraged as it was an excellent means of picking-up quickly, humanely and efficiently. Had I been field trialling, however, I doubt that the judges would have seen it as a good fault!

Generally, however, if left unchecked, this type of behaviour is likely to worsen as the dog becomes older, more experienced and begins to realize that he can get away with running-in. Once the fault is allowed to establish itself, it is very difficult to cure. As in all cases of gundog training, prevention is better than cure and so it is as well to assume that your dog will eventually be tempted and to take preventative steps from the very beginning. To this end, when shooting or picking-up, position the dog in front of you and not to the side. Not only will the dog have a better view and should, in theory, be able to mark birds down more efficiently but it also means that the handler can keep constant watch on the dog at the same time as seeing what is going on generally. The first time you go out as a gun, and if there

is no member of the family available or prepared to come and stand alongside you to hold the dog if necessary, peg the dog down rather than risk him running-in as you concentrate on your shooting.

In early training, a young dog may begin running-in to the dummy and this must be eradicated immediately. Fortunately without the distractions of people and the shooting day, a dog which develops this problem at this stage is easier to cure. You should never persist in throwing the dummy, just to see whether he runs-in again. Throw the dummy as usual but have the dog on a lead or check-cord and

By placing the dog in front of you when either shooting or picking-up, there is a better chance of being able to keep a close eye on the pupil and thus prevent any inclination towards running-in.

tied to a post. When you are sure that he is sitting quietly, go and pick up the dummy yourself. Remember that, in the same way as when you are teaching steadiness, you should walk backwards towards the retrieve keeping an eye on the puppy at all times and being ready to chastise should he attempt to run in as far as the lead or check-cord will allow.

Running-in should not be confused with steadiness, but it may pay to read these comments in conjunction with those concerning *steadiness* (see p.105).

<table>
<tr><td>

TRAINERS' TIPS

- If a dog has started to run-in, he can be cured in the initial stages by discriminate use of the check-cord.

- If schooled properly, this problem should not occur. If it does, get a friend to shoot or throw a dummy, (whichever the animal finds most tempting) at a distance. If the dog runs-in, the friend can pick up the retrieve and you can severely reprimand the dog.

- Make sure that you are positioned between the dog and the direction in which the dummy is to be thrown. Face the dog and sit him down. Throw the dummy backwards over your shoulder. In this way you will be able to cut off the dog should he attempt to run-in past you.

</td></tr>
</table>

SCENTING

I cannot decide whether or not my cocker spaniel bitch has true 'scenting' ability. One minute she goes berserk in my training area, the next she hangs back around my heels.

Obviously such a query leads to the suspicion that the dog is bored. No dog, no matter how keen, can be expected to work continually over the same piece of ground. On the days when a dog shows that extra 'sparkle' on the training field it is likely that a gamebird, or rabbit or even a songbird has been over the ground and the dog is scenting this rather than, as the owner fondly imagines, a dummy. (See also *boredom*, p.14, *lessons*, p.60, and *exercise*, p.36.)

TRAINERS' TIPS

- Obviously both the training area and the exercises the dog is being asked to perform should be varied.

SKIN IRRITATIONS

Is there a readily available preparation with which I can bath my spaniel? I do not want to go to the expense of seeing the vet.

As briefly mentioned in the section dealing with *lice* (see p.61), some gundogs suffer from skin allergies and irritation whose symptoms can be similar to vermin infestations.

Despite the expense, the opinion of

Scratching can be caused by a variety of skin irritations.

a vet must be sought and his recommendations adhered to. It is likely that Alugan will be prescribed for a general skin irritation. Occasionally, Quellada veterinary shampoo will be recommended and this is possibly one of the best as it will eliminate sarocoptic mange, fleas, lice and similar extoparasites. It has a G.B.H. gamma benzene hexachloride BP base.

SNIPE

What is it about snipe and woodcock which makes the average retriever hesitant to pick one up?

Whether it is the scent or actual taste of these two types of wading birds which repels the dog, no one seems to know, but most agree that the problem can be overcome by practice. The difficulty is, of course, in being able to give a dog sufficient practice and thereby experience, due to the fact that both species are relatively scarce on most shoots.

TRAINERS' TIPS

● Peter Moxon, writing *Training the Rough Shooter's Dog*, (Popular Dogs, 1977) suggests:

> . . . practising on dead starlings, using them as you would a dummy; if necessary encased in a nylon stocking. I have invariably found that, once a dog will pick-up and retrieve a starling happily, your troubles are over.

SPAYING

When she last came in season, my German short-haired pointer bitch was nearly 'got' through the garden fence by the neighbour's 'Heinz 57'. Life is so awkward when she comes on heat that my wife and I have been discussing the practicalities of getting her spayed. Could this cause problems and affect her working ability?

First, a well-constructed kennel and run will prevent a bitch being 'got at' when she is in season. Secondly, exercising under supervision well away from other dogs and away from home so that any would-be Romeo cannot follow her scent, would negate the need to consider spaying.

A lot of careful thought must go into the subject before a young bitch is marched down to the vet. What would happen for instance, if once she realizes her full working potential, and proves to be outstanding, you could not perpetuate the line?

There are also several possible side-

A kennel and run may help in ensuring that a bitch in season cannot be 'got' by a wandering male. Think carefully however, before deciding to have a bitch spayed.

effects of spaying, including excessive weight increase and subsequent lethargy which can, in time, affect both training and working ability, possibly even temperament.

TRAINERS' TIPS

● If you decide to do the deed, the vet will advise you of the optimum time for the operation to be performed. This is certainly not before the first season has taken place. My vet prefers that the bitch should have had at least one litter.

● Talk to other trainers and the vet before going ahead with this operation.

STANDING

My spaniel, who has been working for a couple of seasons now, has recently developed the habit of standing on his back legs when working through thick cover. Is this usual or should I consider this to be a fault relating to steadiness or a lack of it?

Trainers have many differing views when it comes to the subject of steadiness: some are happy for a dog merely to halt when required; some wish him to sit or even lie down as they feel this is a further step removed from running-in. (The dog could get up via the sitting position, stand and then move.) Those of the latter thinking would therefore consider standing on the hind legs to be a stage nearer to unsteadiness.

Basically, however, and you should also read the following section on *steadiness*, the only degree of steadiness that is required is one which will ensure that the dog does not spoil the shot; retrieve without orders, nor put up other game either out of shot or, if rough-shooting, while the gun is unloaded. If standing on his back legs is not a signal to the handler that a particular individual is contemplating any of these 'sins', there is no cause for concern.

TRAINERS' TIPS

- Many seasoned dogs, when working in cover over which they cannot see, acquire the habit of standing on their back legs in order to get a better view. I have never heard of any dog being taught to do this. I think that it is hereditary and comes from keenness.

A keen youngster 'pointing'. Like 'standing', it cannot be taught, and neither is a fault provided that they are not forerunners to unsteadiness.

STEADINESS

I am teaching my young flat-coated retriever to sit and stay outside its kennel when I clean it out. Am I being too severe on the dog and should I instead let it have the freedom of the garden?

The ability to sit and stay (and perhaps more importantly, the handler being confident of his dog's ability to sit and stay) is an important aspect and indeed an integral part of gundog training. Only after a dog has learnt to sit and stay should dummy training begin. Without such basic obedience it is but a short step to

Steadiness can be a matter of kennel routine where dogs must wait before being allowed either in or out. Alternatively it can be taught as a specific training exercise.

running-in.

All dogs, but especially those of the retriever breeds, need to learn patience and to sit quietly for long periods of time if they are to be an asset out on the shooting field. The situations where steadiness is essential are numerous but a couple of the more obvious ones would be, first, a heavy drive where many birds are falling and the temptation to run-in is strong; secondly, the pigeon shooter's or wild-fowler's chosen companion would not remain in favour for very long if, after long periods of inactivity, birds suddenly flew over and the dog in question leapt through the hide in eager anticipation before the gun had decided that the flock or skien were even within shot.

General steadiness should begin during very early training. Before a puppy is fed, make sure that he waits a second or two before the plate is put down. Also, always make sure that when a dog is told to sit, it does so until told to move and is not forgotten about until it creeps off through boredom.

It is well worth reiterating that, although at first glance, steadiness (or rather a lack of it) seems akin to running-in, and indeed, an unsteady dog will run-in when you least expect it, steadiness is necessary if you are to avoid several of the many problems already outlined in previous sections of this book.

Making a dog sit for the few minutes involved in cleaning out its kennel is a good idea but this should be done after morning exercise and not before, when it would be unreasonable to expect an energetic dog to sit still prior to running off some of its exuberance.

TRAINERS' TIPS

- I sometimes make the dogs sit and stay in a group while working another some distance away. This teaches steadiness to another dog working and it can even be practised in the garden.

- Most people call the dog to them instead of going to the dog. This encourages unsteadiness and breeds anticipation. Go back to the dog.

  Totally different advice comes from another trainer. He is, however, discussing the next stage.

- If there is a problem in steadiness at a distance, sit the dog, walk several yards away and then whistle or call in the dog. When he is almost up to you, give the 'sit' command. Continue repeating the exercise over a period of days, giving the command earlier and earlier until it is possible to stop the dog at any point between yourself and where he was originally seated. Beware, however, of the dog anticipating the recall and running-in or creeping towards you before he should.

STRAYING

Our dog is kept in the house. Now the warm weather has arrived and the back door is always open, she has taken to wandering off across the neighbour's field. Is the only answer to build a kennel?

The general consensus is yes, the only answer is to build a kennel. Without constant supervision, even a professionally trained and initially obedient gundog will begin to develop faults and cause problems. If the dog is of a good working sort, it will not be long before he is hunting, and sooner or later you will be bound to lose him either as the result of a road accident (for which you as the owner may ultimately be responsible) or, if you live next to a livestock farm, shot for livestock worrying. Even though you or the trainer may have taken every opportunity to encounter geese, chickens and indeed all varieties of livestock during the early, formative months, you can never afford to be complacent.

A dog which is allowed to hunt by himself may eventually find a companion of a like mind and when two or more dogs form a 'pack' they are more likely to take to worrying livestock. Sooner or later, given half the chance, the farmer will shoot the dogs, especially if the livestock in question happen to be sheep and he knows that sheep worrying is a serious problem dealt with in his favour by most rurally based magistrates' courts.

If you live near a shooting estate,

TRAINERS' TIPS

- The secret is constant supervision. This can only be achieved by kennelling.

- If you are not able to give your dog attention because you are busy with something else, then the dog should be put in a kennel or somewhere where he is confined and recognizes the place as his own and will happily settle.

- The answer is, do not leave a dog to his own devices. Dogs are quite happy in kennels as long as a routine is observed and they are let out at regular intervals.

the dog which goes off on his own is quite likely to end up caught in one of the keeper's fox wires, and although in the majority of cases, he will be found safe and well during the keeper's rounds, if a wire is set on a bank, the dog may slip down and strangle himself. If the keeper knows the dog he will, for the first couple of times at least, return the dog but as might be imagined, this action could cause a great deal of embarrassment if the owner happens to be a picker-up, beater or even gun on the self-same shoot. After many hours of worrying and even more early mornings and late evenings, any keeper's tolerance is tested and if he should see or hear a dog in or around his coverts disturbing his newly released poults, he may, understandably, shoot the animal and keep quiet.

STUD-DOGS

Obviously any old dog will not do when it comes to finding a mate for my pointer bitch. What should I be looking for?

No matter how wonderful you happen to feel your bitch is, do not ever be tempted to use her for breeding if it is known that she has a serious fault as breeding will only perpetuate it and the fault will almost certainly appear in the resultant offspring.

You should always keep at the back of your mind the fact that you are trying to improve or, at the very least, maintain the same standard, as there is no other reason for maintaining a particular blood line. Do not fall into the same trap as so many others and think that you are

VETERINARY COMMENTS

Never be tempted into playing 'God', for example by trying to miniaturize a particular gundog breed which has, through generations, become over-large. Putting a large dog to a small bitch may well work once and the breeder may be able to pick out one of the medium-sized youngsters for his future use, but to attempt miniaturization for its own sake will only introduce faults not normally seen in the gundog breeds. In extreme cases, the progeny's body may become too heavy for the leg size as, although it is possible to scale down the particular breed's overall aspects, it is not possible to scale down knees and other joints – with the result that you achieve dwarfism. This type of breeding could cause patella luxation, perhaps better known as 'slipping stifle', most often noticed in ageing dogs of the various terrier breeds by the unmistakeable 'one-two-three, hop' as they walk.

going to make a profit from the eventual sale of the progeny as, by the time they have reached the age of seven or eight weeks, the money which you can ask for the puppies of even the best-bred gundog is not likely to do more than repay the vet's fees and food costs incurred from the rearing of the puppies.

A great deal of thought must go into choosing a dog which will be suitable for a particular bitch and every aspect of its physical make-up, working ability and temperament should be considered. No one, it must be admitted, can prophesy with any degree of certainty the outcome of a particular mating but if there is to be any hope of success, the choice of dog is every bit as important as breeding from the right bitch.

Unless the potential stud-dog is a proven worker, there is a likelihood of the sporting attributes already present in the bitch being weakened. This is where pedigrees and other records kept by reputable breeders come in useful.

Be aware of the difference between line-breeding and in-breeding. Most breeders would advise that the bitch should not be put to any member of her family closer than an uncle as to do more than this results in line-breeding becoming in-breeding and without expert understanding of genetics, which the first-time breeder is unlikely to possess, highly strung, nervy and fault-laden puppies are likely to result.

If the dog's breeding is similar but not too close to that of your own bitch, there is a far greater chance of producing good puppies than if you take the bitch to a completely unrelated stud-dog. Even when it is decided to out-cross, there should still be, somewhere in the pedigree, a dog who is at the very least half-brother to a dog or bitch on the dam's side. In the opinion of most breeders, an out-cross mating should be carried out perhaps once in every three generations as this will retain all the good points already achieved but the new blood will give added strength and improvement to the weakening genes.

TRAINERS' TIPS

- If you, as the owner of a potential stud-dog, are approached by the owner of a bitch and, for one reason or another, you feel that it would be an unsuitable mating, you must not be frightened of saying so.

TAIL DOCKING

Why do spaniel breeds need to have their tails docked as puppies?

The general view is that a working dog, which is required to enter thick cover, will probably suffer more discomfort through the damage caused in rough conditions than it will in the few moments it is necessary to take in docking a young puppy. Whilst most people agree that the docking of all breeds for show purposes should be prohibited, the majority also feel very strongly that the docking of working dogs should continue.

In the summer of 1991, the Home Office, without consulting any gundog organizations, imposed Schedule 3 of the Veterinary Surgeon Act 1966 (Amendment Order 1991) whereby

TRAINERS' TIPS

- Remove half the puppies from the nest, leaving the remainder with the bitch. Take them away before docking just on the off chance that one may squeal and upset the bitch. Once the deed has been done, return this half of the pups and take out the rest taking care not to let any of the puppies be in a situation where they get chilled.

- I would doubt that there is any real need to dock at all, as any undocked spaniel, provided that he is from a working strain, should be as capable of pushing through cover every bit as well as a docked one. Cutting a third off the tail will not, in my opinion, lessen any damage.

after 1 July 1993 it will be illegal for anyone other than a qualified veterinary surgeon to carry out a tail-docking operation. Presumably, this Act will also forbid the removal of dew claws other than by your vet. Most breeders remove these claws (which are found immediately above the foot) at the same time as they

dock, feeling that they serve no useful purpose and could, indeed, cause problems in later life.

Although in view of the new legislation, the Trainers' Tips do not perhaps strictly apply, the differing opinions are, I feel, still worthy of inclusion.

TEMPERAMENT

I have, fairly recently, invested in my first springer after several years of successful experience with labradors and I am anxious to start off on the right lines. In an article I saw, a quotation from an old trainer stated, 'You can train a retriever while feeding the chickens – training a spaniel takes a lot more time'. Is there really that much difference in temperament between breeds?

As I mentioned in the section dealing with a choice of *breeds* (see p.19), the retriever is intended for formal shooting, spending most of the shooting day walking sedately to heel or in a butt or hide, only coming into action when something is to be retrieved. It is, therefore, under minimal temptation to do wrong.

The spaniel, on the other hand, is designed to seek out and flush any game within gunshot. A spaniel works under maximum temptation – especially considering the distance at which he normally operates from the handler.

Common sense therefore dictates that you should assume that, generally speaking, the retriever breeds are more placid than spaniels

which are naturally restless animals, bred to keep on the go all day long.

TRAINERS' TIPS

- Offering advice to novice shooters about which dog they should acquire is never easy, even taking into account the type of shooting most frequently indulged in. Most folk have an inbuilt bias towards one breed or another but do remember that there is a world of difference between the temperament of a labrador and that of a spaniel.

111

TICKS

I am intending to have three weeks on the grouse moor in September and am taking my two spaniels. With the current publicity and research on Lyme Disease, which I understand is transmitted by sheep and deer ticks, I wonder about the danger to my dogs. Should I burn off any ticks found with a lighted cigarette?

At the time of writing, a three-year research programme has just been undertaken which will, hopefully, throw some light on the subject of Lyme Disease. At the moment very little is known save that it is passed on to humans via the sheep and deer tick. The initial symptoms are apparently similar to arthritis accompanied by a feeling of influenza. I personally know of a deer stalker and a game dealer's daughter who have actually contracted the disease through the deer tick. Fortunately, the doctors concerned were aware of the possibility of this disease and were able to diagnose and treat both patients before any serious harm was done. If it is not diagnosed, however, it can be rather unpleasant and so it is as well for anyone likely to be out and about on moorland or similar terrain to be aware of its existence.

Ticks are generally most active during the late summer and early autumn and it will pay the owners of any dogs working in heathery, bracken-infested conditions to keep a close watch around the animals head area, especially the ears and neck. Spaniels, golden and flat-coated retrievers may well, because of their longer coats, suffer from unseen ticks and so it will pay to strip out the ears and neck parts. Although usually associated with the show bench, the stripping out of the worst of the coat will help in detecting the presence of ticks. It might be thought that by trimming out the outer guard hairs, you will also lose much of the essential oils, but it is not the length

When attempting to remove a tick, it is all too easy to destroy the blood-engorged body and yet leave the head firmly encased in the skin. If left unnoticed, it could cause a very bad sore.

Cocker spaniel and unwanted 'guest'.

of the coat which counts but its density. Stripping a rough-coated dog only results in shortening the guard hairs rather than removing them.

At a time when almost everyone smoked, the usual procedure for the removal of ticks was a lighted cigarette to the head of the parasite. As the head is almost always buried in the animal's skin, the nearest you can get is the blood-engorged body. Whilst the application of a cigarette makes the tick shrink and *appear* to drop off, the head will undoubtedly be left in place causing, at the very least, bad sores.

TRAINERS' TIPS

- It is important to ensure that the whole tick is removed. I have found the best way of doing this is by applying a dab of petrol or paraffin onto the tick and then grabbing it with a pair of tweezers before jerking it off with a quick twist.

TRAIL-LAYING

I would like to offer my dog some more stimulating exercises which involve retrieving without constant, and therefore boring, repetition. I believe it is possible to lay trails to improve scenting ability. How is this best done?

Trail-laying is best done by attaching a dead bird or chosen dummy to the centre of a piece of cord and, with the help of an accomplice, dragging it along the ground. The reason for this is that, should you try and lay a line by dragging an object by your side, the dog will follow the handler's scent rather than the one given off by the time it is to be retrieved.

Whilst a retriever trainer wishes his dog to follow the simulated scent of a pricked bird or rabbit, a spaniel owner is probably more likely to want his animal to trace a scent in order to improve his flushing capabilities. Trainers of retrievers and spaniels are not, therefore, necessarily in complete agreement when the subject of trail-laying is broached.

As Talbot Radcliffe, writing

Laying a scent trail by means of string and dead pheasant.

Spaniels for Sport (Faber and Faber Ltd, 1969) says:

> Some trainers avoid trails altogether and consider their own foot scent an efficient substitute. Some never lay them with the retrieving bundle, but wait until such time as the puppy has had his first lessons in retrieving the real article and lay them with that. Others lay them with a bundle slightly scented with aniseed, while some lay the retrieving bundle pure and simple.
>
> In deciding for yourself this question of laying your trails you must remember that you have to train your spaniel to ignore most foot-scents when he is hunting. Consequently, you must have some means of teaching him, on receiving the appropriate command, to change his tactics when you wish him to pick up and follow the foot-scent of wounded fur or feather.

TRAINERS' TIPS

Changing from the usual format, this topic is best covered once again by a quotation from *Spaniels for Sport* in which Talbot Radcliffe offers the following trainer's tip. (Also, refer to *mouthing* p.67.)

> Although the ability to take your own foot-scent at a gallop may be of some value, it leaves much to be desired. Various methods have therefore been adopted with the object of avoiding confusion of your own scent with that of the object dragged. It may suffice, for a time at least, to get someone else to drag the object in an ordinary manner. Let him get well away before you bring up your dog. On the other hand . . . simpler still, you can attach the object to a fishing rod by a short piece of string and by this means trail the object at a little distance from your own foot-scent, but if you desire to make assurance doubly sure, get someone else to lay the trail with this.
>
> If it appeals to you, you can teach your dog to go back for anything that you have dropped, whether he has seen you drop it or not . . . Drop the object, at first in his sight and afterwards unknown to him, and take him along with you for an ever increasing distance before you send him back for it. This is said to cultivate the memory. It is certainly most useful in hurrying up a dog that is getting slow in his return, for he will not like being left behind. This method also considerably improves a tender mouthed dog that tends to keep dropping the object on the return journey.

TRAINING EQUIPMENT

As a novice gundog trainer. I wonder what artificial equipment is needed.

All gundogs, no matter what breed, need to respond to the commands given via the whistle. The need for various actual training aids and equipment depends to some extent upon the breed and the type of work a dog is expected to fulfil.

Apart from whatever type of *whistle* is selected (see p.139), a lead will be needed. Its use in training a puppy to walk to heel or to stay is obvious but too many people tend to leave the lead behind once the dog is trained and working. The cord type of slip-leads take up very little room in a coat pocket and should be kept in the shooting jacket to be used at the beginning of a shooting day; between drives and perhaps even as a restraint whilst shooting when your concentration is on the gun rather than the dog. Using a lead is not, as so many seem to feel, an indication of a badly trained animal; in fact it is more likely to impress than a dog allowed to run off and/or begin self-hunting.

Some owners use a piece of apparatus similar to an over-grown corkscrew which is screwed into the ground and the lead attached. These can be slightly cumbersome and, in my opinion, are not strictly necessary as there is bound to be a tree root, log or gun peg to which your dog could be attached. Always be on the look-

out for potential danger, however, and never tie a dog where the lead could trip up the handler as he turns and swings onto a bird. I used to see some guns with their dogs tied to their coat or gun belt but this habit seems to have become less prevalent as these handlers have realized the danger of being tied to a dog which may at any time move suddenly due to excitement or over-keenness to pick-up.

Dummies are obviously essential to the trainers of retrieving breeds as well as to most spaniel handlers who will, at some time in their lives, require their dog to pick-up. Whether you buy purpose-made canvas dummies or make a selection at home matters little, but whereas canvas dummies can only be of differing sizes and weights, a home-made selection

If some form of restraint is felt necessary, a cork-screw type tether is cheap to purchase and safe to use.

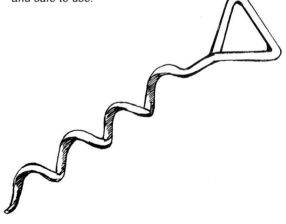

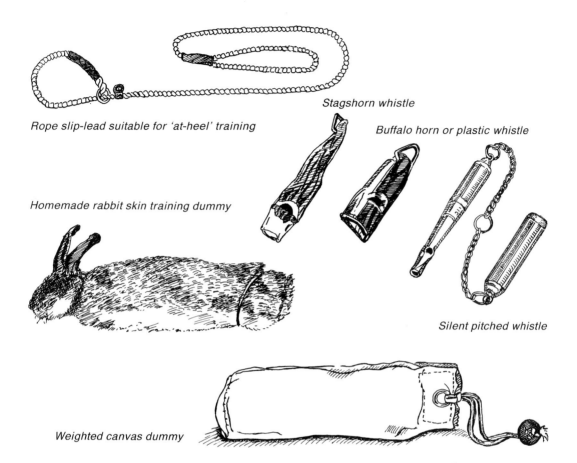

Rope slip-lead suitable for 'at-heel' training

Stagshorn whistle

Buffalo horn or plastic whistle

Homemade rabbit skin training dummy

Silent pitched whistle

Weighted canvas dummy

can encourage a puppy to pick first a rolled-up handkerchief or woollen sock before progressing to rabbit skin or wing-clad offerings thus simulating the aspects of retrieving most likely to be encountered on a shooting day.

The professionals differ in their opinions of starting pistols. Most believe that because of its 'crack', rather than a 'bang', its use should be moderated. A dummy launcher sends off the dummy with a starting pistol crack and so you must assume that these too must be used carefully bearing in mind the fact that the noise may upset a gun-nervy or sensitive puppy.

A selection of training equipment which should be sufficient to begin the education of a young dog.

TRAINERS' TIPS

- We are not very fond of starting pistols and dummy launchers as we find that these tend to make a lot of dogs gun-nervy. We much prefer a small-bore shotgun.

- Items like check-cords should only be used by people who know how to use them.

117

TRAVELLING

I have no trouble in getting my dog into the car – in fact my problem is just the opposite! He is very keen on travelling but I cannot make him sit quietly.

It is far easier to train a gundog to sit quietly in a car than it is, say, a terrier. (The latter's favourite stance seems to be with their hind legs on the front passenger's seat, front paws on the dashboard and nose pressed up to the window!) A gundog, being more biddable, should do as he is told and provided that early training has been carried out, there should be no problem in insisting upon discipline whilst travelling.

Although it should be possible to allocate a dog a particular portion of the car (the floor well of the passenger side for example), it is perhaps better if you either buy or construct some form of travelling box which will fit on the back seat or in the boot of an estate car. Not only will this keep the car clean and prevent the dog from moving around, but the dog will also be happier in having a small mobile 'kennel' of his own.

When I used to travel a lot – loading for my employer and taking my dog with me – I found that a hessian sack was a good way of ensuring the dog did not spread mud and dust all over the interior of his Jaguar XJS! The dog in question soon became used to being picked up and placed in the sack with only his head protruding. A piece of baler twine

It is far better to allocate a small portion of the car specifically for the dog rather than expect him to be happy wedged in alongside the rest of your shooting equipment.

Although beyond the financial reach of most, a specially constructed trailer is undoubtedly the answer to any travelling problems.

tied loosly around the collar area prevented the sack from slipping and it was equally as effective as purpose-made (and expensive) travelling bags available on the market.

If the journey is a long one, remember to stop at intervals and give the dog a drink from the water bottle carried with you. Travelling seems to dehydrate a dog more so than if left in kennels or at home. Food is not so important. In fact, a dog should not be fed during the journey and should have very little, if any food at all before embarking. It is far better to wait until you reach your distination when a bowl of food will help a dog settle into his new surroundings.

Dogs can be encouraged to travel in a car at an early age and with pleasurable activities. It is important that a young dog is always taken to an enjoyable venue so that it realizes that travelling invariably means fun.

TRAINERS' TIPS

● If a dog is reluctant to travel, try leaving the back of the car up (if an estate or hatch-back) so that he can get in or out at will. Feed him in the car in some cases.

● Never put a dog in the boot of an ordinary car as they can suffer from exhaust fumes. Make or buy a special box. If you have more than one dog and do a lot of travelling, consider investing in a trailer.

TRAVEL SICKNESS

I have tried feeding my dog in the car. I have also tried taking him on short journeys and then, as soon as he gets out of the car, giving him a retrieve so that he associates travel with pleasure. Unfortunately he still suffers from travel sickness.

When I first purchased the dog mentioned in the previous section he was, despite the miles which he eventually travelled in later life, very prone to sickness. In fact when, as a young keeper, I brought him home from the breeder, I was stopped by the local police for not displaying my tax disc. Upon being stopped, the pup threw-up over my legs and I was allowed on my way by a very sympathetic police officer! (As an aside, the tax disc was in the glove compartment.)

Despite gradual acclimatization to the vehicle, feeding in the back and being given interesting runs after short journeys, he could never settle and it was not until I sat him on the passenger-seat floor area, where he could not see the immediate surroundings, that he began to relax.

Feeding a dog before travelling will not help any feeling of sickness and it is far better not to give any food at all.

TRAINERS' TIPS

- I always use a cage in the car, as this protects both the dog and the car. The dog is less likely to get thrown around during transit and it also seems to eliminate travel sickness.

- If all else fails, consult your vet and use travel sickness pills available from him.

A specifically constructed box forms the ideal mobile kennel and can help in eliminating travel sickness.

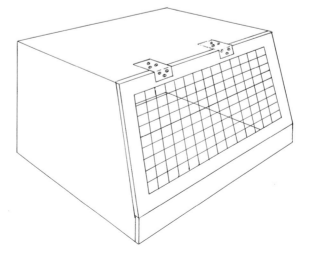

U

UNDERSHOT JAW

I keep both gundogs and terriers. Any book dealing with either topic mentions undershot and overshot jaws. Is it possible to clarify exactly what is meant by these terms?

When choosing a puppy, you should – amongst many other things – check that the puppy has neither an undershot nor an overshot jaw; that is, where, when the teeth are closed, one set is either slightly in front of or behind the other set. This is easily done by gently lifting back the lips whilst holding the jaws closed.

To clarify the matter further, an undershot jaw is one where the bottom set of teeth protrudes in front of the upper set. Conversely, an overshot jaw will show the upper set protruding further than the lower casing.

As you check for these problems in a puppy, you should also ensure that the teeth are clean and that the upper lip is pink. The latter fact usually indicates that the puppy is in good health.

TRAINERS' TIPS

- You should not breed from a dog with this problem.

UNDESIRABLE HABITS

Everyone recommended that we kennel our seven-month springer pup. Unfortunately, she has begun the rather unpleasant and undesirable habit of eating her own faeces.

Although not an uncommon habit, it is indeed undesirable and, to humans, disgusting.

The cause may be due to a heavy worm infestation, a lack of minerals and/or vitamins in the diet (see the sections on *feeding* p.38 and *vitamins* p.127), or merely boredom. It also suggests an irregular exercise routine (see also *exercise*, p.36 and *dirty kennels*, p.32) as no dog enjoys dirtying his immediate environment and would much prefer to empty himself well away from home.

TRAINERS' TIPS

- Anything not in the training schedule is an undesirable habit but we suggest a regular worming routine in this particular instance. Feed a well-balanced diet.

- Increase the amount of exercise given, particularly after meals so that the dog is encouraged to keep a clean kennel.

- Depending on what food is being given as the day-to-day diet, it may pay to change over to fresh butcher's meat if you are feeding either an all-in-one meal or the normal tinned meat and biscuit. Whatever is being fed; add a teaspoon of dried yeast to each feed.

UNSTEADINESS

My spaniel is, at the moment, perfectly steady and I trust him to do everything asked of him. I intend to start beating on a local shoot and do not want all my hard work to be spoilt by the other beater's badly-trained dogs and, as has happened in the past, when working my old dog, the keeper putting more and more responsibility on me.

In an ideal world, you should be able to exercise every care during a dog's first shooting day and thus avoid any temptation towards unsteadiness. In real life, however, it is not possible to order the rest of the line to work at a slower pace so that your own spaniel never misses game nor has the inclination towards running-in as he sees a shot bird drop at the end of the drive.

Some do's and don'ts may help. Never send a dog to retrieve immediately the shot has been fired. Never send a spaniel to hunt in the same direction in which a bird he has just flushed has gone. It encourages unsteadiness as, in the dog's mind, he is heading for the original quarry.

If a dog shows the least inclination to act without orders, do not let him go until you have come up to him and given your usual command. Never call him back as this will induce a further degree of unsteadiness. Go back to basics and forget about formal work if this is felt to be detrimental to the animal's future. It is far better to miss a few days in the first season than have to miss a decade through eagerness.

If your dog, though steady, is getting sloppy in his retrieving, only hunt him often enough to keep his hunting right. Use him as a retriever whenever opportunity offers. (Refer also to *steadiness*, p.105 and *running-in*, p.97.)

TRAINERS' TIPS

- If it is the first time on a shoot, do not expect the dog to behave as well as he has during training. If it is the subsequent years that you are worried about, never expect your dog to be as good as he was at the end of the season before. Put him through a modified course of handbreaking before the season opens; you will save much loss of time and temper, and the possible ruination of your dog.

- If the line is going too fast on the dog's first day, put him on a lead rather than risk a chase and the breach of rapport which ensues.

- If a dog reverts on the shooting field, go back to early training. Correct unsteadiness by 'sit-and-stay' exercises and always make sure that the dog is put back exactly where he was left. Use a marker to ensure that the correct place is maintained. Walk away from the dog backwards with the hand outstretched.

VACCINATIONS

Is it necessary to vaccinate my gundog? I never intend to enter field trials when, if what I have been told is correct, I would need to vaccinate in order to compete.

It is absolutely essential that all dogs (not just the gundog breeds) are vaccinated and that their booster jabs are up to date.

Initially, two injections are given, one at around about eight weeks and the other after an interval of around 14 days. These vaccinations should

---

TRAINERS' TIPS

- If a dog is to be used in any form of competition, the governing body will insist on up-to-date vaccinations and will state it on the schedule.

- It is perhaps more important to ensure that a country-kept dog is vaccinated correctly than it would be for one which is kept in town and gets a chance to build up a certain degree of natural immunity from constant contact with other dogs. Rats in the

country mean that a dog is more likely to get leptospiral jaundice if the boosters are not kept up to date.

- Older dogs do build up a degree of natural immunity but I still have all my dogs 'jabbed' each year. In fact I have negotiated a special rate with my vet for doing my dogs *en bloc*. This cuts down on a little of the expense.

protect the dog against distemper, hardpad, leptospiral jaundice, virus hepatitis and parvo virus. Booster doses are then required every 12 to 24 months, or as advised by the vet on the vaccination certificate.

As will be seen in the veterinary comment regarding *weil's disease* (see p.134), immunity to leptospiral jaundice does not persist for as long as some of the other diseases that can be vaccinated against, so be sure to clarify the dates of each and every subsequent booster injection with your local vet.

VISION

I am intrigued to know whether there is a fundamental difference between canine and human visual apparatus and if not, would I be safe in treating my dog's eyes as I would my own when problems occur.

Like cats and horses, but unlike humans, dogs have a third eyelid. This comes across the eye from the front corner to protect it. Rarely, cysts may develop within this eyelid, and it is not an uncommon site for malignancy. Any swelling in this eyelid should be treated with suspicion, and veterinary advice sought. The third eyelid can be stitched across the eye and, in this way can provide both support and

VETERINARY COMMENT

- Excess watering of the eye can be a sign of periodic ophthalmia. If there is a thick or pussy discharge, it is most likely that the dog has conjunctivitis.

- Brambles and hedgerow sticks frequently damage the front surface of the cornea and injuries vary from a superficial scratch to complete penetration and rupture of the eyeball. Such injuries are always serious, and a vet should be consulted straight away. The healing of corneal wounds is slow because there are no blood vessels in the cornea. These must 'grow' in from the side of the eye. After healing, a permanent scar, visible as a white spot, will remain. Unless very large, these do not usually affect the dog's vision.

protection for wounds to the front of the eyeball while they heal.

Conjunctivitis is quite common and often occurs as a result of dust, brambles or bedding entering the eye. As with human conjunctivitis, the condition should respond rapidly to treatment with antibiotic eye ointments and bathing of the eyelid with cotton wool and warm water.

If one eye is weeping excessively, it may have been injured, or once again, a foreign object such as hay-seed or a fly may be irritating it.

VISITS TO THE VET

My wife says that I am worse with my first gundog puppy than ever I was with our children! I hear so many stories from friends, however, as to the fear their dogs show when going to the vet for injections and routine check-ups that I wonder how these problems can best be avoided.

A dog which is used to people and is confident in their company should be well able to cope with a visit to the veterinary surgeon. We have recently had a German Shepherd dog in our kennel which required a visit to the vet for suspected ear mites. Upon informing the owner, his first reaction was one of horror and secondly a request to warn the vet of her unpleasant nature. In actual fact, the visit went without mishap and the bitch in question was as pleased to see the surgeon as she would have been to see her dinner plate. It is all a question of confidence; had we been nervous (as her owner obviously is), this would have been transferred to the bitch.

Advances in the veterinary field over the last 20 years or so have been most impressive. Improved drugs (particularly antibiotics and vaccines,

TRAINERS' TIPS

- The owner should make a point of getting to know his chosen vet. This need not be the local surgery; the owner or trainer should find a veterinary practice which shows an obvious interest in the kennels and the animals kept therein. In return, as soon as the vet sees that the owner really cares, he will do his best and no problem will be too much trouble.

as well as surgical techniques) have made life much easier for dog owners in general and gundog owners in particular. Thanks to the combined injections against distemper, hepatitis, jaundice and parvo virus, these diseases no longer pose the threat that they once did. The isolation kennels used by responsible professional trainers means that they are well able to deal with any trouble immediately it becomes evident. (A dog going in for training will, therefore, be kept separate for a time and this will ensure that no inherent disease can be transferred.)

Visits to the vets should cause no problem to the average working-bred and well-trained gundog.

VITAMINS

Is it necessary to add vitamins to my dog's food? As recommended, I use an all-in-one type.

Provided that a balanced diet is being fed, there should be be no reason to supplement an animal's food with vitamins. It is only when an unbalanced feed is given that problems will arise.

A prime example of a particular dietary problem occurred several decades ago when it was noticed that some herding dogs in Northumbria were beginning to suffer from an ailment known as 'black tongue', the cause of which was at first unknown but eventually it was realized that the problem arose at exactly the same period as rabbits began to suffer from the first-ever bout of myxomatosis. At the time, it was common practice for shepherds and farmers to feed their animals nothing but flaked maize. The dogs had, however, been augmenting this rather meagre diet with rabbits caught during the course of their work and these had given them the necessary proteins and vitamins to remain healthy and hard-working. The absence of rabbits destroyed this balance between meat and cereal and, as a result, the dogs became ill.

Despite a balanced diet, it may, however, be necessary to include multi-vitamins in the diet of a pregnant bitch. These should be fed alongside additives of both calcium and phosphorus.

TRAINERS' TIPS

● Beware of adding too much cod-liver oil in the diet of a whelping bitch; too much will induce symptoms similar to rickets.

VOICE

I am beginning to realize the importance of whistle commands and hand actions now that I have begun serious training but find it difficult to encourage my dog by the tone of my voice. Am I likely to run into problems because of this?

There are certain people with whom dogs have a certain empathy and no one can be really successful in gundog training unless they are one of these. The hunting fraternity call this 'weaving the thread': hunting patois for the empathy of the dog man to his dogs.

One of the key ways in which a huntsman weaves this thread is by communication. Sometimes he can get his hounds to move almost by telepathy; at other times his tone of voice gets across exactly what is wanted.

Voice is therefore very important and especially so during the early training of a gundog. A soft tone of voice can encourage or reward. If it is harsh it can upset very sensitive dogs, but those of an extrovert nature will need to be handled in a firm tone.

People who cannot alter the tone of their voice (perhaps they are embarrassed to make a fuss in case some onlooker overhears them) will undoubtedly have problems in training.

TRAINERS' TIPS

- If you feel it is a serious problem and you cannot 'talk' to your pupil, go and watch a field trial. The successful dogs will know what is required of them and whether they have done the right thing by listening to the handler's tone as he speaks.

- Never nag a dog continually or he will soon learn to 'switch off' and not listen to you. Give the command in the right tone and you will see whether or not the dog has understood by his tail action and eye expression.

- It is not the command that is important but the tone in which it is delivered.

- Never shout or get over-excited when giving commands.

A huntsman can only hope to control the vast number of hounds in his charge by means of his voice. Likewise, a gundog handler who can encourage and discourage by voice alone is more likely to be successful than one who cannot.

WALKING TO HEEL

I have a Welsh springer which I cannot get to walk to heel properly when off the lead. We start out well but as the exercise progresses. I end up almost running to keep up with the dog's ever-increasing pace.

Not only will a dog sometimes refuse to walk to heel when off a lead but sometimes he will walk perfectly on grass but not in roots. In all cases, it indicates a lack of early training and a

Lessons in walking to heel should begin when the puppy is quite small. Avoid potential problems by ensuring that the dog is 100 per cent on the lead before progressing to the next stages. (Always be sure that the lead is currently applied as shown in fig on p.23.)

necessity for more practice.

Initially, training should begin by walking the dog on a slip-lead (never a choke-chain). If the pupil pulls, or alternatively lags behind, a quick tug and the command 'heel' will, in most cases, have the desired effect. 10 to 15 minutes' heel-work each day should soon have the dog walking well on the lead. After a few sessions of this duration it should be possible to allow the lead to drag on the ground before eventually removing it completely. The pupil should by now, in theory at least, be walking to heel properly.

With a dog from a working strain there should be no need to bother with anything other than a normal slip-lead and certainly no necessity for aids such as the Halti, which the manufacturers claim will make a reluctant dog walk to heel.

TRAINERS' TIPS

- Use a slip-lead high up on the dog's neck behind the ears. Give short, sharp jerks, and never drag a reluctant dog. Only start work off the lead when you are 100 per cent sure that the dog is perfect on.

- Go back to heel-training as described in all the usual gundog books. Try walking the dog against a fence or hedge if you think that this will help your particular problem. Use a 'swishy' stick and tap the dog's nose if he walks too far in front.

- I have found that most dogs walk well to heel if you walk with the flat of the hand just above the dog's head. As with hand signals, the white palm seems to focus the animal's eyes and attention.

- After getting to the stage when the lead can be allowed to drag on the ground, I then tie the lead up around the dog's neck before finally taking it off.

WATER WORK

We perhaps chose the wrong dog from a litter of working labradors. She was neither bold nor the runt of the litter but is, it has to be said, of a sensitive nature. With time and perseverance from both my wife and myself she has mastered all the aspects of training so far expected of her. She is not, however, as forward in her training as shooting friends and training books suggest she should be. Having got this far. I now want her to enter water and subsequently retrieve from the same. Please advise as to the best way of introducing her to this new element without frightening her.

Most working-bred dogs take to water as a matter of course. Continual walks which include messing about around the water's edge will eventually result in a little exploration and before long, the

Choose a sunny day and shallow water before attempting to introduce a young dog to this new element. Handlers who are prepared to take to the water themselves will help in showing the pupil that there is nothing to fear.

puppy's natural curiosity will compel him to swim out in order to investigate a floating lump of wood or similar object.

The actual entry to water should be taken gradually. If you are fortunate enough to have a stream passing through the area in which you normally exercise, a young animal should soon become accustomed to following the handler backwards and forwards across water. The great thing, however, is to show by example and also to use only shallow water to begin with.

If the correct and necessary bond between dog and handler has already been created during earlier training it should, quite literally, be but a small step before you can begin to wade through even deeper water yourself knowing that the pupil is confident enough to follow. When he eventually becomes confident enough to use water as he would the land, a dummy retrieve can be introduced. Starting at a very easy range, the distance should be gradually increased until the dog is swimming out as far as the dummy can be thrown.

At this stage, it is very useful to be able to include narrow stretches of water and throw a retrieve onto dry land on the opposite bank. The puppy has then to swim before concentrating on questing for the retrieve in reeds or thick undergrowth. Such training is especially important in cases where a dog is eventually to be used in searching for wounded duck, for example. (See also *wildfowling*,

p.141.) In such situations, long retrieves over big stretches of water should also be practised. Throw the dummy down-wind and let it drift to further and further lengths before the dog is sent, until a naturally bold animal is quite happy to swim enormous distances. Talbot Radcliffe, writing in *Spaniels for Sport* (Faber and Faber, 1969) states that he believes, 'it is just as easy for a dog to swim as to walk and that really long distances over water never fatigue a dog'. He also states that, 'with maturity, a body build-up and age, a dog will stand any reasonable amount of work in its second season. If a dog is kept exclusively for water work, it is advisable for him to keep in a much fatter condition than you would for land work. The coating of fur does seem to help in warding off the cold.'

Returning to the subject of retrieving from the opposite bank, this often presents a young dog with unsurmountable problems unless specific training has been included as part of the overall training programme. The natural water current will obviously present difficulties to a youngster whose immediate reaction will be to swim and fight against it. Experience will, however, tell him to note the approximate point of retrieve before swimming across the current and landing down-stream.

If water is likely to be a constant obstacle in your chosen sport, it might pay to take this already advanced stage of water-work just one stage

TRAINERS' TIPS

- I have yet to find a dog that is actually scared of water; it is usually a lack of confidence in his ability. Some dogs of a sensitive nature will be somewhat shy of water but perseverance will pay off.

- Use shallow water, go out with the animal and encourage him. An older dog

where available will prove to be a useful teacher, but never be tempted into throwing a reluctant pupil into water. This really will result in a pupil who is frightened of water permanently.

- Start when the weather is hot. Do not hurry the pupil.

further and ask a friend or assistant to position himself on the opposite side of a large stretch of water in order to throw a dummy a greater distance than your own capabilities will allow. By using the chosen command to retrieve, the dog will

very quickly learn that a retrieve awaits it on the opposite bank.

Early and gradual introduction to water is essential when training the wildfowler's dog. Throw dummies to the opposite bank of a narrow stream at first before going on to the 'real thing'.

WEIL'S DISEASE

What are the dangers of my labrador picking up Weil's Disease when out on a shooting day?

In actual fact, Weil's Disease is one of the two forms of leptospirosis and is only known by this name as and when it affects humans. Dogs can get leptospirosis, and it is known as leptospiral jaundice or, colloquially, 'lamp post' disease.

Lamp post disease was common until the arrival of modern-day vaccines and this particular strain (which affects the animal's kidneys) although a problem was nevertheless, fairly easy to cure. In some cases however, victims were left with chronic nephritis.

The second strain (causing Weil's Disease in humans) attacks by infecting the liver and is potentially more dangerous, leading to jaundice. Unfortunately, it is frequently fatal.

Every dog owner should be aware of the seriousness of leptospirosis and there is indeed an ever-present danger to dogs working in the countryside. Terriers are perhaps the working type most likely to suffer as they are known to be very efficient at catching rats and it is generally thought to be rats which are the main reservoir of infection.

TRAINERS' TIPS

- As leptospirosis is generally picked up through infected rat urine, if a dog shows signs of jaundice – namely yellow discoloration of the skin and mucous membranes – avoid contact with the dog's urine in case the infection is present. Make an appointment with the vet. Better safe than sorry.

VETERINARY COMMENT

Immunity to leptospirosis does not persist for as long as some of the other diseases that can be vaccinated against. Whereas you can get away with boosting the immunity against those a little late, it is wisest to keep your appointment for a jab against this infection.

WHELPING

My bitch is pregnant. I have followed the various advice given to the letter, including feeding twice daily from six weeks into the pregnancy, ensuring that she is receiving plenty of vitamin D, and giving her a course of multi-vitamins to help redress any natural imbalance in the food. Having got this far, I have no wish to risk any problems with the puppies by making a mistake on the whelping day itself.

Before whelping day, the bitch should be made acquainted with her whelping box which can be made from plywood or plain boards laid together to make a platform sufficiently roomy for her to stretch at full length. The box should be raised three inches from the floor level and provided with a wooden lip on the outer side which should be about six inches in height.

When several dogs are kept, try and kennel the in-whelp bitch well away from the others and the resultant distractions, especially if this is the first litter. Whelping in maiden bitches is frequently accompanied by restlessness for as long as 48 hours

An easily constructed whelping box. Avoid problems by: (a) making sure that it is roomy enough for the bitch to lie out at full length and; (b) that she is happy to use it as a bed well before the day the puppies are due. The actual dimensions of the box obviously depend upon the breed and size of the bitch in question. An added refinement is the anti-crush bar.

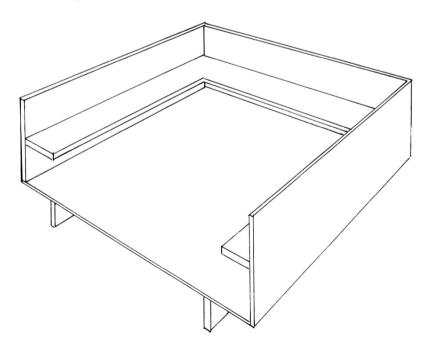

before commencement. Such animals should be given plenty of time to settle – lay out some newspapers in the box so that she can scratch them up together and make a nest. These can be burned after the puppies are born and replaced as often as necessary.

The first pup should arrive about two hours after real labour pains have first been noticed and the intervals between the puppies can be most irregular. If you are on hand (and it is advisable during the first whelping) and there has been an interval of more than four hours since the last puppy but the bitch is obviously in some discomfort, indicating that there are more pups to come, the vet should be called as there could be a puppy

VETERINARY COMMENTS

Worm the bitch either before mating or very early in the pregnancy. Roundworm larvae lie dormant in the bitch's bloodstream, only becoming active again when she is pregnant, and they then enter the body of the foetus via the bloodstream.

blocking the entrance to the cervix. A greeny-coloured discharge which suddenly appears may indicate that there is a dead puppy inside and once again, the vet must be called immediately.

The bitch should, by instinct alone, chew through the umbilical cord and, provided that she is not too upset by your presence, you should move the puppies closer to her head so she can lick them off and stimulate them into life. She will probably attempt to eat the placenta and should not be discouraged from this as it is thought that it contains certain nutrients which aid the milk-flow.

TRAINERS' TIPS

- The bitch should, from now on, be fed on high-protein feeds if she is to provide sufficient milk for the puppies to do well.

WHINING

Perhaps I have chosen the wrong breed as all my shooting is done from a peg. Nevertheless, I have an English springer who is an excellent retriever and adds greatly to the enjoyment of my day. Unfortunately, on a 'heavy' drive, (we shoot about 300 pheasants a day) she tends to squeak and whine. I saw an article in the Shooting Times *which suggested an old, cleaned-out washing-up liquid bottle filled with water and squirted at the dog would cure this problem but despite my wife's effort whilst I was shooting, we did not achieve the desired result. My spaniel is totally steady and even when at 'squeaking pitch', never attempts to run-in.*

In the opinion of the experts, this problem is usually caused by too early an introduction to the 'real' thing. Although spaniel breeds are generally accepted to be a little more excitable than the more placid retriever types, the problem of whining can be found in any breed. All trainers agree that it is a very hard fault to correct and suggest that, should the dog in question be used by a forward-standing gun who is therefore 'close to the action', you should give up the gun until the problem is solved.

No potential gundog should be taken out on a shoot until he is at

Some claim to have had success in curing a whining dog by squirting water from an old washing-up liquid bottle every time a 'squeak' is heard.

least 18 months old. I know that many readers will disagree with this statement and be able to quote examples of a 12-month or even younger animal performing well on their local shoot. Two of the litter sisters of the cocker bitch which I am currently training were in the beating-line at the age of eight months and, having seen them work, could not be faulted.

At this age, however, they are still too young and 'puppyish'. Without intelligent handling and very great care they will, I am sure, develop problems as a result of being placed under stress at too early an age.

TRAINERS' TIPS

- Have this potential problem (along with all the others) at the back of your mind at all times. Get all the basic training done first: sitting and staying and, most importantly, stopping on the whistle. The dog can then be sat on a drive or two but not right up with the guns. He should not be allowed to retrieve until he will sit quietly and calmly through a drive. Do not sit a dog through a 'heavy' drive at first and always leave the dog sitting, picking up any fallen birds by hand so that he does not begin to anticipate being sent for a retrieve. One or two retrieves may be allowed later.

- Take advantage of a shooting friend and volunteer to pick-up for them before taking a dog out on your own shoot. In this way, it is possible to stand back and negate any possible temptation which may in turn lead to whining.

- If the problem occurs, give the dog a complete break. Start again from the beginning, keeping well back from the line of guns. Give no retrieves which the dog has watched come down. One or two from cover will be alright.

WHISTLES

Please recommend the best type of whistle for use when training gundogs.

Unfortunately, no manufacturer of gundog whistles has, as yet, come up with a magical type which will create instant obedience in a dog the first time he hears it. Many would-be trainers do, however, seem to think that their particular whistle possesses certain powers and are disappointed when the pupil does not behave in copy-book fashion.

The first requirement must be to teach the dog whistle commands and teach them thoroughly. If you ever reach a point where a young animal ignores the whistle it is more likely to be as a result of confusion rather than defiance.

It is easy enough, for example, to have a dog which will return quickly when three 'pips' on the whistle have been blown. The average dog only takes a few short lessons to realize that given a verbal command, hand signal and a long blast on the whistle, it is expected to sit down. Initially, this will be done with the dog at heel or at least in close proximity to the trainer. But, just when you are confident enough to blow the 'stop' whistle at a distance, the pup comes rushing back instead of dropping. It is a test of the handler's patience not to be annoyed by the fact the puppy is, in his mind at least, coming in response to the whistle and is not being disobedient. Never, ever punish the dog for returning: if you cannot make it realize what is required by a

Before using any whistle (no matter what type is eventually chosen) the young dog must be confident enough in his relationship with the handler. Initially, crouching down will encourage the pupil to respond to the 're-call' whistle.

firm hand signal, a verbal command for 'down' and a stamp of the foot, go back to basics rather than risk losing his confidence in you.

Start by blowing the 'stop' whistle whilst the pupil is at heel; then with a free-running lead. Build up gradually until it is obvious that each step has been understood.

It is amazing the number of differing opinions the seemingly unimportant subject of varying whistle types evokes. On the one hand, a particular trainer tells you not to use a metal silent whistle as it soon becomes full of spit; on the other, another trainer says that a silent whistle is ideal for spaniels. Yet another despises any form of metal whistle because of the tendency for them to freeze to your lips on a cold winter's morning.

The third obviously prefers a whistle made either of stagshorn or of buffalo horn, but the one who says silent whistles clog up with saliva dictates that plastic is the best as, should you lose the original, it is a simple matter to buy a replacement of exactly the same tone. Stagshorn- and buffalo-type whistles are, in his opinion, made individually and no two whistles are alike. In practice, I have found that it is the way in which the whistle is blown and the lung power used which dictates my dog's response and, upon panicking on a shooting day and inadvertently blowing the wrong whistle as the dog is heading towards disaster, the usual series of blasts creates the same,

TRAINERS' TIPS

- Use one of the plastic variety. They are in fact, colour-coded and numbered in tone so that should you lose one, it is a simple matter to replace.

- We use buffalo horn; it holds its tone well. Too many different tones will cause confusion.

- I use an ACME 211+ without a pea and a silent whistle for spaniels. I find these two whistles adequate for all types of gundog training.

favourable, reaction.

Once you have brought a dog into the shooting field, no matter in what sphere, there is the danger of forgetting the artificial whistle. No keen sportsman sleeps the night before a shooting day. If he is a shooting guest then he has to think of the locality of the scheduled meet, the inclusion of his gun, a plentiful supply of petrol and sufficient funds to tip the keeper. A beater or picker-up needs to remember waterproofs, stick and dog. A lead and a whistle are also required but, being such small items, they are easily forgotten.

A dog which is trained to respond to natural mouth whistles is, therefore, a useful asset, as you have the advantage of never being able to forget your mouth! Once again, you may encounter problems on an icy cold day when, no matter how hard you try, a pair of pursed lips will not utter a single audible sound.

WILDFOWLING

Up until this year I have relied on the services of my friend's two dogs for picking-up whilst wildfowling and duck flighting. Two seasons ago, I lost several shot and wounded birds through not having a dog close enough to pick them up immediately. In an effort to remedy the situation I bought a spaniel and, come September, will be taking her with me. How can I look after her when fowling so that she does not succumb to health problems later in life?

Whatever faults spaniels may have, generally a fear of water is not one of them. They have a good undercoat, well protected by harsh guard hairs,

Old hessian sacks will break up a light coloured dog's outline, making it less easily seen by incoming wildfowl. They will also help in drying a wet animal.

and can withstand most of the hardships the coast and marsh has to offer.

Although outwardly wet and bedraggled, if you were to take the trouble and feel through to the soft undercoat, you will notice that it is warm and dry. This does not mean that they can be expected to withstand long periods in freezing conditions and icy water. This is indeed folly and is bound to result in problems later in life.

A good shooting companion is a rarity and his working life is all too short, so it is in the owner's best interest to care for the animal to the best of his ability.

A supply of hessian corn or flour sacks is a useful addition to your wildfowling equipment. They can be used as a makeshift hide, protective cover for a light-coloured dog and either a dry mat on which the dog can sit or a rough towel with which to dry the animal at the end of flighting.

TRAINERS' TIPS

- I have found that in very cold weather standing and waiting in 12 to 18 inches of water for any length of time puts a spaniel (or indeed any other breed) out of action. It appears to paralyse them across the loins and will in my opinion, invariably result in arthritis or worse. Make every effort to leave the dog on dry land unless actually retrieving. When I used to be involved in duck-flighting, I had an old van and used to put half a bale of wheat straw (not barley as the 'whiskers' tend to get in the dog's ears) in the back. By the time I reached home, the dogs had dried themselves off. I also used it as a kennel when staying overnight but the odour and condensation in the morning has to be seen and smelt to be believed.

- Beware of encouraging running-in when wildfowling as this could cause problems in other forms of shooting you may wish to undertake. To avoid this, don't send the spaniel immediately, but do send him quite quickly as crippled duck diving in open water form a difficult retrieve if valuable time is wasted. A good dog soon learns the difference between wildfowling and situations where he must remain either in a pigeon hide or until the end of a pheasant drive.

WORKING TESTS

I have been attending training classes for several months now and as an end-of-term exam, it has been decided to hold a working test. We are apparently having two stakes; Novice and Open. (I am told that this is to cater for all levels of dogs within our group.) Although I have not yet experienced a sleepless night through worry, I would appreciate knowing something of the type of test my golden retriever will be asked to perform.

Gundog classes and working tests are undoubtedly a good thing, as not only do they allow people who otherwise through day-to-day circumstances would be prevented from indulging in the sport but they also act as an excellent stepping-stone to the more formal and exacting field trials.

A list outlining the requirements at a working test for retrievers can be found in *Gundogs; Training and Field Trials* by Peter Moxon (Popular Dogs Co. Ltd). Basically they consist of:
1. Dog walking to heel 100 yards.
2. Dropping and remaining down whilst handler disappears from sight

Whether at a club test, working test or gundog scurry, always listen carefully to instructions. Many points can be lost by bad handling.

100 yards away.

3. Handler reappearing and recalling dog.

4. Retrieving hidden dummy from cover.

5. Retrieving dummy over three-foot jump.

6. Two dummies thrown up 80 yards out, one to the right and one to the left, each being saluted with gunfire. Dog to retrieve only the dummy indicated by judge, ignoring the other.

7. Retrieving from water, or from cover on the far side of a stream or river.

Some of the clubs also include temptation for the dogs in the form of a rabbit pen containing live rabbits, a dummy being thrown in and the dog being expected to retrieve this whilst ignoring the rabbits. Tests for novice dogs are made somewhat simpler.

Provided that the dog has had a thorough basic training, none of the above should cause too great a problem. What is likely to be more difficult to overcome when first considering entering a working test is 'stage fright'. A great many handlers,

because of nerves, tend to over-handle their dogs with the result that they transmit their own nervy state to the dog which then reacts in one of two ways. Either he goes wild, forgetting any earlier training or he just will not go at all, sticking round the owner's heels.

TRAINERS' TIPS

- Working tests are another reason for joining a gundog club – they keep the interest going during the summer months when little else is happening.

- It is not a good idea to enter working tests once your dog is entered to the shooting work, as I have noticed that too much attention to artificial work and a continual use of dummies tends to bore an experienced dog often resulting in a loss of pace and style.

WORMS

Worms and their elimination are obviously an important part of gundog care. Have you any information or tips which may prevent health-care problems?

Regular worming is extremely important and a broad-spectrum wormer, available only from vets,

should be used in preference to an 'over-the-counter' preparation which is generally not so effective.

The regular diet must be considered before deciding on the type of worm most likely to affect your particular dog. Tapeworm, for instance, is more readily found when uncooked meat is the main source of dietary income and the flesh of sheep has been found to contain more than its fair share of tapeworm-inducing ingredients. Hookworm is particularly common in hunt kennels but hardly ever found in pet animals or gundogs. It is an interesting fact that foxes may act as reservoirs of infections, since the rate of the worm found during experiments has been as high as 91 per cent in some areas.

An infection of one thousand larvae has been found to give a hound diarrhoea and smaller infestations are associated with a leakage of protein into the gut which then shows in the hound by means of digestive disorders and a generally poor condition. In severe cases, it may show itself further with lesions on the feet and skin where the paws become swollen and deformities of the pads and claws can develop.

Infection larvae can develop anywhere where there is sufficient warmth and moisture. The development of the egg is influenced by weather conditions, and accounts for the fluctuation in the number of worm cases seen as the overwintering larvae die away in the spring or early summer to be replaced by a new generation, with peak numbers occurring in high summer.

Two more common helminths known by all dog owners are the tapeworm and the roundworm, both of which are parasites of the bowel but which, in kennels maintaining a good standard of indoor hygiene and a regular worming programme, should not cause any serious problem. Sometimes, a gundog is found to be a host to 'whipworm' but once again a broad-spectrum wormer should prove to be an efficient form of eradication. The egg is, however, very long-lived and if a grass run should happen to be used, it could prove to be a potential source of infection for at least five years – another good reason why kennels and runs should be based on concrete.

It is often tempting to include a grass exercise run where space permits, thinking that it gives one or more dogs the choice of constant exercise. It does but perhaps the disadvantages outweigh the advantages and it is an undoubted fact that the transmission of these internal parasites is facilitated by the aggregation of numbers of dogs sharing grass exercise runs. Where these are used, every effort should be made to clear the runs of excrement regularly.

The question of worms affecting humans should never be underestimated and both roundworm and hookworm can be a serious problem in this quarter. *Homo sapiens* become infected by ingesting the sticky, embryonated eggs found in faeces or dust which have contaminated his fingers or food.

Grass exercise runs are, admittedly, more common in hunting establishments than they are in the gundog world. If, however, you decide on a grass run for your dog, beware of the increased danger of worms and parasites.

When man ingests the embryonated ova of any form of toxocara, hatching inevitably takes place and the larvae will invade the tissues of the body. Although humans do not function very efficiently from the parasites' viewpoint, as most of the intermediate forms in human tissue are sterile and incapable of infection, hookworm differs. (Remember, though, that it is an infection rarely found in the ordinary breeds of gundogs, so there is no need for any undue alarm.) It will affect the lungs and liver plus, in certain circumstances, the spleen, kidneys and bone marrow, leaving a hydatid cyst for which at present the only feasible remedy is surgical removal. Tapeworms also use man as an intermediate host and the result of such activity may show as one of these cysts.

Children are well known to suffer from worm-induced diseases and the probable reason for this is due to the fact that they cannot be expected to maintain a high standard of hygiene normally carried out as a matter of course by adults or older teenagers.

Lungworm, although not common in dogs in Britain, is often first noticed by coughing, which some supposed experts put down to kennel cough. In actual fact, from the veterinary point of view, 'kennel cough' is an ailment which may have several different causes, only one of which is found in the trachea and bronchi, particularly at the point where these join together. Many cases are without symptoms but infection is sometimes characterized by a chronic dry cough, exacerbated by exercise, which occasionally ends with a retching action. It seems likely that the larvae of lungworm are transferred by an adult bitch, which is not noticeably affected, licking her offspring.

Finally, it is often assumed that, just because a dog rubs its bottom along the ground, he is suffering from worms. In actual fact, this behaviour is more likely to be due to impaction or infection of the anal glands, which are needed by dogs in the wild to mark their territory. With domestication they have obviously outlived the use of their glands, and it is best to let the vet express them.

TRAINERS' TIPS

● Worms are usually associated with general health problems, including poor coat, unusual appetite amongst other things. Obviously the best plan is to worm the dog at regular intervals so that these problems do not arise.

● I use an all-in-one worm tablet which eliminates 90 per cent of all worms including roundworms (the commonest) and tapeworms.

● I do not think that a worm problem would ever affect training but a bright, healthy dog is obviously better material with which to work.

When worming your dog, no matter what the breed, make sure that the wormer has been swallowed. Many animals become adept at spitting out tablets once the handler's back is turned.

WOUNDED GAME

I have been asked picking-up by our local keeper. In the past I have seen wounded game killed by all kinds of methods. What do you consider to be the most humane way of doing this and can you see any problems which wounded game may cause to my labrador?

Wounded game and *hard mouth* (see p.47) quite often go hand in hand. If a dog refuses to pick wounded game it could be for a variety of reasons: inexperience and confusion upon coming across a retrieve that flaps and moves; being put on to wounded birds at too early an age; or due to being 'spurred' by a previous retrieve (see *retrieving*, p.91).

Wounded game should not, however, cause any problem if the dog is introduced to the situation in the right way. Once a dog is competent at picking cold game he should be introduced gradually, allowing only one or two retrieves on dead game out in the open. Once this is achieved, the number of retrieves can be increased over a period of time until he is retrieving say, purely as an example, ten a day, spread over several drives. Occasionally do not allow the dog to pick up at all on a drive. If you explain to the 'captain' of the picking-up team that yours is a young dog and you have no wish to jeopardize all the early training, he is sure to understand, and the rest of the team will be only too pleased to cover for you. (Never be frightened of saying 'no' to a gun who may ask you to go for a pricked bird. Likewise,

explain to him that it is your first time/season out and you have no desire to rush things. Only a fool would take umbrage at your refusal and if you are picking-up on a shoot where these are to be found, then you would be better employed elsewhere.)

There is an understandable desire for any dog handler who witnesses a strong runner fall in full view and then 'leg it' for cover to send his dog immediately. Logically, it makes life easier to pick-up such a bird as it falls rather than risk losing it in dense cover. Resist this urge, as sending a dog for running bird which falls in full view results in unsteadiness.

Undoubtedly the most efficient way to despatch game is to dislocate the bird's neck, but this method is frowned upon on most shoots as, unlike chicken which, once dead, are hung by their feet, game is hung by the neck in order that the blood remains in the chest cavity and both flavours and tenderizes the meat as it hangs. Traditionally, game is tied in 'braces' by string around the neck and an efficient shoot will have both a game cart fitted with racks and game-cart driver who will brace, sort and carry the shot birds to the larder. With game prices being as low as they currently are, it is folly to risk damaging birds unnecessarily by merely throwing them in the back of the beater's trailer or in the Land Rover where dogs and boots soon flatten them beyond recognition and cover them in mud. No game dealer in his right mind will give a good price for such offerings when the shoot next door presents him with clean, dry and well-hung game. Wounded birds which have had their necks broken are more susceptible to falling from the rack as the neck bone is already damaged and the string cuts around the skin which is the only material attaching head to body.

There are on the market, various forms of patented killers which claim to kill wounded game both quickly and efficiently, but I do not know of anyone using them on a regular basis. A fisherman's 'priest' may be the answer but the majority of these do not have a heavy enough weight with which to kill an old cock pheasant.

Most pickers-up carry a stout walking stick and this is arguably the best way of despatching wounded game. By holding both wings in one hand at the point where the wings join the body, a live bird will push its head forwards. A single clout at the base of the skull and at the point where the head joins the neck will, nine times out of ten, cause immediate death and is so much better than the various ineffective and therefore inhumane methods you sometimes see on shoots.

Never, ever forget that once you reach the shooting field, each retrieve which the dog brings to hand was, or perhaps still is, a living creature and should be dealt with as such. There is a world of difference between a canvas dummy and a pheasant or hare.

TRAINERS' TIPS

- Too much work on wounded game can make dogs ignore dead birds, preferring instead, the excitement of the chase.

- Not only can wounded game cause a dog to become unsteady or begin to be hard mouthed, but ground which contains hares and dogs which are permitted quarry, may result in a wounded hare actually ripping open a dog with its strong back legs.

- The dog's first retrieve of wounded game should be on a bird that is not going to run but which is, nevertheless, still alive. He will usually accept such a retrieve and will graduate to runners with experience. Never send a young dog for a runner until the bird has reached cover. Not only will this prevent the onset of unsteadiness but it also prevents the chasing of unshot game.

WOUNDS AND SCRATCHES

Since seeing a friend's springer spaniel rip the fleshy interior of its hind leg when jumping a barbed-wire fence, I have kept a canine first-aid box alongside mine in the car. It contains: a pair of surgical scissors, crepe bandages, elastoplast rolls, cotton wool, a packet of lint, and an antibiotic aerosol spray. I have just realized, however, that apart from the latter item, I have nothing to deal with wounds and scratches and if I had, I am not sure that I would know how to treat deep or infected wounds.

Whether a wound is best stitched or not is a decision for the vet and will depend on how fresh it is, its depth, and its position on the dog. (Wounds on the head and body heal well; those on the limbs tend to be less successful.) If the wound is fresh, it is best not to touch it at all before the vet has given his opinion. It should not be washed with disinfectants because these can damage the tissues and reduce the healing capacity. Clean, lukewarm water can, however,

Because of their long ears, spaniels are more prone to wounds in this area than are any other breed of gundog. Regular inspection and bathing after each outing are essential if you are to prevent infection.

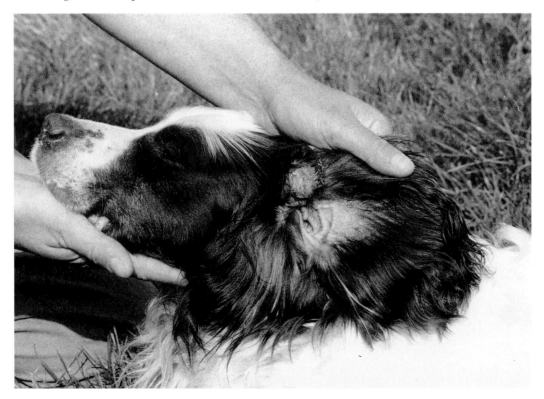

be used to cleanse the wound and lint applied to a leg wound (under a bandage) for the trip to the veterinary surgery.

If the wound is not fresh (12 to 24 hours old), it will already be contaminated with bacteria from the skin and so there would be very little point in stitching it as that would seal in the infection rather than eradicate it. Contaminated or deep wounds can be cleaned and washed with cotton wool and a solution of mild medical disinfectant. A suitable antibiotic ointment (ask a vet) should be applied.

Deeper wounds on certain parts of the limbs could involve damage to important inner structures. These are serious injuries – it may be necessary to stitch together tendons that have been completely severed. It is therefore obvious that there should be no delay in seeking veterinary help if it is suspected that these deeper structures have indeed been damaged.

VETERINARY COMMENTS

The most important point when treating wounds is to keep them clean and dry. Whether a wound is best stitched or not is a decision for your vet.

An animal which is constantly working could benefit from the use of a liquid antiseptic upon reaching home each evening. Gundogs with rough or woolly coats could receive wounds which, because of the thickness of the coat, may go unnoticed so the use of an antiseptic such as TCP or Savlon will prevent these injuries from festering.

XENOPHOBIA

The problem with my dog is that she appears to have a total dislike of strangers.

A dislike of strangers (xenophobia) is not uncommon in a dog of a sensitive nature. Unfortunately, a nervy or sensitive dog found in normally placid gundogs breeds will often cope with xenophobia by attacking first in order to protect himself. Highly strung and interbred breeds such as German

TRAINERS' TIPS

- A nervy or sensitive dog which is frightened of strangers should have plenty of time spent in building up his confidence and overcoming this fear. This is one instance where a dog would benefit from being kept in the house rather than a kennel so that he has ample opportunity to meet visitors, hear the phone, radio and television, as well as becoming accustomed to the banging and clattering of kitchen utensils.

- If, however, a dog shows a dislike of people then it must be taught that familiarity breeds contempt and taken on as many trips to shopping centres, country fairs and indeed any other well-populated venues as time and necessity allows.

- Don't give up. With experience a dog should overcome this dislike of strangers.

Shepherd dogs tend to be more guilty of this kind of behaviour than do the normal gundog types, although it has to be said that the occasional labrador has been known to go 'off the rails'.

If you are unlucky enough to own an animal which does turn vicious and cannot be trusted with people or dogs out on the shooting day, then there can be no alternative but to have him destroyed. There is, however, a world of difference between a vicious dog and one which occasionally fights (see *fighting*, p.41).

YAPPING OR YELPING

Occasionally, my spaniel has been known to yap from excitement when a pheasant or rabbit gets up at close quarters.

This problem has been dealt with under *whining* (see p.137) but in the case of a spaniel where the training in the introduction to live game has been rushed and the dog has subsequently been allowed to chase live game, this usually results in the dog giving tongue.

TRAINERS' TIPS

- See the section on *whining* and adapt the solutions offered there.

- Very difficult to cure once the fault has occurred – sorry I can't be more helpful.

ZEALOUSNESS

No matter how much exercise or work my cocker spaniel bitch gets, she never seems to tire and I always come home from either walking or shooting feeling that she could do the whole thing once again.

Part of the charm of a fit, healthy and well-trained spaniel is this zealousness and general eagerness to please.

The entries under the letter Z in the *Pocket Oxford Dictionary* could have been written with an eager spaniel in mind covering, as they do:

> Zealousness – Earnestness or fervour in advancing a cause or rendering a service. Hearty persistent endeavour. Extreme partisan or fanatic.
> Zest – Keen enjoyment or interest.
> Zing – Vigour, energy.

What better definitions can be found to describe an ideal shooting companion, bred from working stock and trained to pefection?

TRAINERS' TIPS

- Zealousness can never be classed as a fault and zest or zing are assets which merely require channelling into the right activity.

CONCLUSION

THE FUTURE OF SHOOTING AND ITS CONNECTION WITH TRAINING

Field Trials, their format, rules and method of marking an individual dog were originally derived as a means of testing an animal's suitability to the shooting field. The series of tests are supposed to simulate events and happenings which could occur during an ordinary day's shooting.

Whilst field triallers who train a dog purely to compete and be proficient in the same undoubtedly exist, it is more likely that the majority of competitors are shooting men and/or women for whom a well-trained dog adds to their day's pleasure. On my own particular estate, some regular beaters and pickers-up also have shoots of their own as well as competing in field trials. Their dogs are, of necessity, true 'all-rounders', aiding both my employer and myself, their handlers on their days and being sufficiently disciplined to justify consideration into a field trial draw.

The connection between shooting and gundog training must never, therefore, be forgotten and it is interesting to see that an independently produced survey on the economic and conservation significance of country sports published in February 1992 emphasized the fact that total direct expenditure incurred by the organisers and participants in hunting, shooting and fishing has risen by 40 per cent in the last ten years.

Logic dictates that this increase has been generated by an upsurge of interest in all fields. Whether as a result of political moves, greater potential leisure time or higher wages matters little so long as field sports continue to contribute towards conservation and the creation of countryside features.

Much of this contribution is made voluntarily and at no public cost.

Eighty-two per cent of landowners cited game coverts as the reason for retaining or planting small woods.

The current popularity of field sports in general and shooting in particular must be due in no small way to it becoming a diversion more and more accessible to the general public. The more that the population is encouraged to shoot the more gundogs will be needed (and the more answers to potential problems in whatever context will be required!)

According to the Cobham Report, 'Interest in countryside sports continues to rise and the participants and supporters of countryside sports continue to be drawn broadly from the different socio-economic groups'. Proof indeed that gundog users need not necessarily be ultra-right wing. Conservative-voting members of the land-owning fraternity.

Field sports contribute a total of £459 million towards central and local government; 22 per cent of which comes from shooting. Expenditure is more than that spent on books, live arts and the cinema. It is also equivalent to a least 10 per cent of the weekly consumer expenditure on leisure (excluding motoring.) Whilst field sports in general fall behind walking in popularity, they are equal to golf, football and swimming and are well ahead of both cycling and riding.

---

*Countryside Sports: Their Economic and Conservation Significance –
Commissioned by the Standing Conference for Country Sports, prepared by
Cobham Resource Consultants*

A NOTE ON FEE-TAKING TRAINERS

Suitable for some, especially those with full wallets, I personally feel that, by sending one's own dog away for training, the actual owner and eventual handler is missing out on the pleasures which can be obtained from training a puppy from scratch. It is often said that the novice will ruin at least one dog before successfully training a second or even third 'attempt'. Unfortunate though it may be for the first pupil; not being allowed to realize its full potential through nothing more than mere ignorance, the observations noted and experience gained are undoubtedly valuable lessons to be learned and cannot be achieved second hand.

Before going any further, I have to say that I have no wish to decry professional trainers; dogs are their life and any one trainer is likely to have experienced more fads and foibles of both owner and puppy alike in a single year than I have in twenty years of bringing on a pupil for either myself or my employer – after all, this particular book would never have materialized were it not for the favourable and business-like answers to my perhaps, occasionally naive questions. Those who have chosen to risk making a living from a potentially hazardous vocation and in many cases, agree to a mortgage with no real idea as to their income two months' hence, have to be doing it for the love of gundogs rather than for any real financial reward.

Some people have genuinely not the time to properly train a young dog and they will have no alternative but to send a dog away for training or buy a 'ready-made' adult animal. For humane reasons if nothing else, a dog brought on by someone else is better than no dog at all. Without a dog on a shooting day much valuable time is wasted whilst the gun explains to a picker-up exactly where the pheasant fell, and the direction it took as a pricked bird.

FUN AND FROLICS

Although we would all like our dog to be a potential Field Trial champion, all that is really required is one which is obedient, understands regularly given commands and is reasonably proficient at aiding the handler in his chosen aspect of shooting. An over-simplified comment certainly but enough hopefully to take the mystery out of training and put the emphasis on the fun aspect.

After all, your dog is not just a bird finding/fetching machine; it is part of your family demanding almost the same time and attention as a child. The days it is actually working are small in number compared to the total number in a year and yet it requires exercise and a little on-going training during the close season if it is not to develop bad habits and problems. Despite the commitment needed on the part of the handler, keeping and training any dog should never become a chore for if it does, the pupil will sense it and in turn, lose some of its initial 'sparkle'.

Never even consider training a dog unless *your* mind is ready and willing. Going through the motions in a foul mood with no thought of 'fun' is doomed to failure. Contrary to the opinions of many, it is not absolutely necessary to train a dog every day, indeed, to prevent boredom, it is often a good idea to have an occasional break from lessons throughout the most intensive part of its formative training. Use these to broaden the pupil's education in other ways: outings in the car or to the sea are two examples of achieving experience and fun for both dog and handler.

Finally, although I believe that I have, with the help and advice of trainers mentioned at the outset, covered most if not all of the difficulties likely to be encountered, I am, however, willing to bet someone, somewhere is, at this moment, trying to cope with a nationally unique problem. To him or her I apologize and wish them luck! If on the other hand, this book has helped just one person overcome just one seemingly uncorrectable fault and thereby achieve a greater level of enjoyment from both his/her dog and their sport, then it will all have been worthwhile and may go some way towards repaying the immense pleasure which gundogs have given me over the years.

FURTHER READING

Providing a 'bibliography' through which the would-be trainer patiently wades, can be overwhelming due to the fact that opinions on basic training vary tremendously and could well result in the reader obtaining too many conflicting views. Some guidelines are, however, obviously required and, in the absence of a local trainer who could offer 'on-the-spot' advice, a carefully chosen book on the subject will provide an excellent reference and a means of step-by-step training.

Although there are many books dealing with the training of specific gundog breeds; arguably the best 'general' book on the market covering almost every aspect must be, *Gundogs: Training and Field Trials*, by P R A (Peter) Moxon. First published in 1952, revised and reprinted on many occasions up unto the present day, it remains for many, the 'Gundog Trainer's Bible'. At the very least, it should form part of any handler's library.

Some of the country/field sports orientated magazines include either a regular page on dog training and associated subjects or feature individual trainers and their particular methods.

In its current format, *The Shooting Times and Country Magazine* seems to be the most suitable periodical for the gundog handler. Its contents vary from shooting, rearing, gamekeeping and stalking through to a full and well patronized 'classified' section, all of which provides the reader with varied views on what should be expected from the beaters and their dogs; the duties of pickers-up and the perils of a poorly trained animal in the shooting line. The classified pages give an up-to-date and therefore realistic indication of prices to charge if one should happen to have a litter of puppies for sale; training equipment or kennels to buy or merely an address from which one can purchase a wad of pedigree certificates or a pair of boots similar to those worn by a fellow competitor at last week's working test venue!

INDEX

As this book has been produced in an A–Z format, an index may seem somewhat superfluous. There are, however, several subjects not covered within a specific main text sub-title and, conversely, some not mentioned in the index due to the fact that they are given prominence on the *Contents* page. It is suggested, therefore, that the reader consults both *Index* and *Contents* when searching for a particular reference and/or problem.